M000195418

For There is Hope for a Tree,
if it is Cut Down...

JOB 14:7

BE
STRENGTHENED
WITH
ALL MIGHT

SAMUEL FATOKI

CREATION
HOUSE

BE STRENGTHENED WITH ALL MIGHT by Samuel Fatoki
Published by Creation House
A Charisma Media Company
600 Rinehart Road
Lake Mary, Florida 32746
www.charismamedia.com

Design Director: Justin Evans
Cover design by Lisa Cox

Visit the author's websites: Samuelfatokiministries.org; Everlastinglife.org.

Library of Congress Cataloging-in-Publication Data: 2014943331
International Standard Book Number: 978-1-62136-780-2
E-book International Standard Book Number: 978-1-62136-781-9

First edition

14 15 16 17 18 — 987654321
Printed in Canada

CONTENTS

INTRODUCTION

THE JOURNEY OF life is laden with ups and downs, but the strong prevail at all times. The joy of a believer is that strength is available to him in Christ Jesus. Nevertheless, as with all gifts from the almighty Father, strength is receivable only by the one who is willing. The believer must be willing to receive the strength, building himself up with all the resources available in God's kingdom.

The book *Be Strengthened with All Might* is Apostle Samuel's charge to all believers to appropriate this special blessing of God. Colossians 1:11 admonishes believers to be "strengthened with all might, according to His glorious power, for all patience and longsuffering with joy." Jesus received all power in heaven and earth at His resurrection and He makes this power available for every believer to stand strong. No believer should lack the strength to live a fruitful and meaningful life.

You will find a lot of scriptures in this book, for it is in the Word of God that the greatest strength of the believer lies. As many of the scriptures you can make personal to yourself (either through memorization, or better still, constant confession), I encourage you to pursue it with keen interest. Moreover, there is a section given to praying at the end of each chapter. These sections are labeled "Praying Points" because they are activity sections: give time to pray! The content of each chapter should encourage you to partake in that activity to complete the blessings that God wants to impart to you through the chapter.

In order to help the reader make the utmost use of the book, there are various subsections in each chapter. The idea behind this structure is to ensure that the reader is able to conclude the reading activity as conveniently as possible, given the usual busy day that men go through today. The opportunity is there to do a meaningful reading in between diverse schedules of the individual. It is not only fulfilling to the reader, it also allows him to digest in bits the information being presented to him; besides, it encourages him to come back to the book for more dosage of the good food for his soul.

It is my sincere belief that you shall be fortified and enhanced to fulfill your destiny through this book. You are more than a conqueror and an overcomer through Christ who loves you!

Chapter 1

STRENGTHENING THROUGH DIVINE PRESENCE

God Is With You

Yea, though I walk through the valley of the shadow of death, I will fear no evil; For You are with me; Your rod and Your staff, they comfort me.

—PSALM 23:4

STRENGTH IS A quality in a man's life that needs to be exercised. You do not really know how strong a man is until there is work to be done and that strength is brought forth to fulfill the task. Oftentimes, however, a man may have the strength resident within him but he is unsure of whether it will save the day. There is no greater assurance needed in such circumstances than the knowledge that God is with you.

If God is with you, you do not need to fear. Fear paralyzes a man from attaining what is needful. Fear sends a message of incapability and unworthiness. Fear hints at the possibility of shame or ridicule coming to you if you dare step out. But knowing that God is with you rids you of the fear.

If God is with us we do not need to fear. The "fear of

evil" is something very real in the world today. Some fear heights, some fear darkness, some fear pregnancy, and some even fear what they know not—psychologists have helped them put a name on it: free floating anxiety! Fear is a torment and God never wants any child of His to live in fear of anything. God has not given us the spirit of fear, but of boldness, love, and a sound mind, the mind of God to think through situations.

God being with us suggests a closeness that is comforting to the believer. The believer should seek greater closeness with God to the extent that he can say confidently that God is with him. This closeness is meant to be enjoyed by the believer as a guarantee of well-being.

God wants to protect and guide us all the way. I love the phrase "all the way" because it is an expression of unceasing, unending, constant protection and guidance. The psalmist, David, could confidently confess that in the midst of the most dreadful circumstances he would fear nothing or nobody. The assurance of God's divine presence gives him comfort, and this gives him strength to pursue the action that he could have been deterred from performing through fear of evil.

You Are in His Hands

> For the life of every living thing is in his hand, and the breath of every human being.
> —Job 12:10, NLT

As it is written in Genesis 2:7, man became a living soul through the breath of God that was breathed into his nostrils. Thus we see that the breath of every human being is originally from God.

God is the One who gives life and breath to every man. Right from conception a fetus enjoys this breath through his mother in the womb, and when the child is born he is preserved by that breath. All through life he is sustained by the breath, and only when he leaves this world is the breath departed from him and returned unto God the Giver.

Since the life of man is held in his breath and breath is from God, the vital issues of life are held in His hands too. A man is able to pursue the activities of life as long as breath is in him. When the breath is taken away, all activities cease. It therefore stands to reason that the One who gives the breath is also the One in control of all activities.

The good news is that God cares for you and He holds your future securely. Before you were formed, He ordained a glorious destiny for you. While you are living it out, He continues to watch over that which He has prepared for you. You can dare to believe that your future is secure in His hands.

You Are Secure in His Hands

In His hand are the deep places of the earth; The heights of the hills are His also.

—Psalm 95:4

There is nothing hidden from the eternal God who has been from eternity past to eternity future. The existence of the world is His thought and His handwork. He's got the whole world in His hands.

Nothing is beyond His reach and influence. Kingdoms and empires, thrones and dominions are all known unto

Him. The fall and rise of empires and kingdoms are known unto Him. As the Scriptures say in Acts 15:18, "Known unto God are all his works from the beginning of the world" (KJV).

If the entire world is in His hands, how then can you think you are beyond His reach? He has got you and me in His hands as well. Before we were formed in the womb, He knew us. He ordained the destiny that each of us lives out on earth.

So rest secure, knowing that you are in His hands. He will never let you fall. Nothing can pluck you from His hands. He said concerning the prophet Isaiah in the Book of Isaiah chapter 49 and verse 16 that his walls are continually before Him and that he is graven in the palms of His hands.

Your God Is With You and He Will Help You Bear the Load

Blessed be the Lord, Who bears our burdens and carries us day by day, even the God Who is our salvation!

—Psalm 68:19, AMP

Just think about it: God carries you day by day. In spite of man's tendency to think himself as important and beyond help, the almighty God knows our frame—that we are dust and that we need help in one area or the other. Before the Ancient of Days who has no beginning we are all children, and He is willing to bear us in His arms.

Hence you are not alone any day. He is there by you to bear you up. But are you willing to let Him? How often does the heart of an adult reach out to the little child that stretches out her arms to be carried? Will you let God carry you? The story is told of a woman with a load on her head who was waiting for a bus to take her to her village. Then came the bus, and the woman boarded but insisted on carrying the load on her head, even though the trunk of the bus had space for the load!

Your God is with you and He wants to help you bear the load. If He has you in His hands, then He's got your entire load in His hands as well. Just as an adult recognizes the load that is beyond the capacity of a little child to bear, so does your heavenly Father. Whatever load is labeled a burden is far too convenient to carry; give it to Him.

This should give you a reason to rejoice! I know there are people whose job is to carry burdens for a fee in some communities, but hardly have I met anyone whose love is to carry burdens. Even beasts of burden like asses often bow the knees under the weight of the burden. Burdens are lifted at Calvary; give yours to Jesus.

YOU ARE NOT ALONE

> For this God is our God for ever and ever: he will
> be our guide even unto death.
> —PSALM 48:14, KJV

You are not alone. Whatever road you travel, you are not alone. Whatever circumstance you are in, you are not alone. He promised that He will never leave you nor forsake you. This should give you strength in all situations.

You have a heavenly guide. Travelers who come to a new environment seek the help of a guide, if they are wise. You are a pilgrim here on earth and you need a guide also. How often have you gone on a journey either within the city or outside and you had to use your GPS because you did not know the way? Imagine what happens when you turn off the GPS! You will go in circles and get into dead ends. God is willing to guide you through your life journey.

You do not need to do the journey of life on your own. When the children of Israel were about to journey through the wilderness, God said that they had not travelled that way before so He gave them the pillar of fire by night and the pillar of cloud by day to guide them.

You can call on Him to guide you. In every step you want to take in life, call on Him to guide you. Are you considering a job or career, moving into a new neighborhood, embarking on a business venture, seeking a life partner in marriage? Whatever decision you need to take in life, He is waiting for you to invite Him to lead you on.

I Will Come to You

> I will not leave you as orphans [comfortless, desolate, bereaved, forlorn, helpless]; I will come [back] to you.
>
> —John 14:18, amp

God's promise to you is that He will never leave you. Fate often deals a person cards that make even those who are relations to abandon or deny knowing him or her. Circumstances in life sometimes make an individual be sorry for his life. Notwithstanding the ordeals of life, there is an anchor that holds sure all the time, and that is God.

An orphan is a child who has lost both parents. The care of such a child is no responsibility of anyone. Unless such a child is adopted by an adult he or she is indeed helpless and miserable. This is the ugly picture that makes your heavenly Father make a sure promise not to leave you.

To be an orphan is to be truly alone. Beyond the provision of food and clothes, there is the emotional need of a child that is significantly unmet in the orphan. We hear stories of abject maltreatment of orphans in the hands of those who foster them. Where the feeling of being loved is missing, the child still feels miserable. Hence, above all it is God's love that He promises us.

God undertakes not to leave us as orphans. He says, "I will come to you!" He understands the timidity and reservations with which an orphan accepts offer for help, but He will break through and reach out to you.

He Is For You

> But the Lord stands beside me like a great warrior, and before him, the Mighty, Terrible One, they shall stumble.
> —JEREMIAH 20:11, TLB

God is not against you. One of the names of God is the Lord of hosts, and as a general of generals He can be fearful and terrible; but the joy of the believer is in knowing that God is for him and not against him. The one that God is against has every reason to quake in fear, as it is written that God merely touches the mountains and they smoke. Therefore every adversary of the believer is in deep trouble because God is against them.

But as for the believer, the Lord is with you and He is for you. He is with you in the moves you make; He is with you to order your steps; He is with you to give you confidence; He is with you to give you cover. He is also for you and will make sure that your projects and activities succeed. His backing makes even the most timid to receive boldness.

The Lord stands beside you like a great warrior. Warriors are fearless and are not intimidated by challenges. A great warrior is renowned for his exploits and conquests. With the Lord standing beside you, enemies think twice before challenging you. The one who dares to resist you does not live to tell the tale. If you happen to be rascally like some spoiled children are, you even taunt the enemy to dare come against you. Such was the confidence of David, and Goliath would find out too late that the Lord who stood beside David is a great warrior.

The Lord is with you and He will never leave you.

God Is For You and He Will Be With You Always

> What then shall we say to these things? If God is
> for us, who can be against us?
> —Romans 8:31

As it is presented in the previous section, God is not against you; believe me, He is not anti-you. Some people have come into situations so deplorable time and again that they feel God is the problem rather than the solution. Such people are religious and have calculated that whatever measure of service they have rendered to God, either in financial terms or other means, such a service should have brought God to their rescue. You need to have an understanding that God can never be on the side of evil. He cannot be bought over, cajoled, or intimidated to side up with the devil. The devil and God are ends apart and have not a remotely tiny area of comparison.

God is not waiting for you to fall or fail. He is not sneakily plotting for your defeat so He could say, "Ha-ha! I got him." He is compassionate and infinitely good, and He is for you. The spiritual forces of evil recognize who God is, and when they know He is for you, they give way! That is why David declared confidently in Psalm 23:4, "Yea, though I walk through the valley of the shadow of death, I will fear no evil: for thou art with me; thy rod and thy staff they comfort me" (KJV).

God is good. He wants you and me to experience His favor and kindness. Even when we are faced with daunting challenges, His favor and kindness always save the day. Boldly declare right now, "The Lord is with me!"

GOD WILL BE WITH YOU ALWAYS

"Fear not, for I am with you; Be not dismayed, for I am your God. I will strengthen you, Yes, I will help you, I will uphold you with My righteous right hand."

—ISAIAH 41:10

Don't be afraid and don't be discouraged. The question often arises in the heart of a man: "What if God does not show up for me?" But God is always there with the comforting words that you should not be afraid or discouraged for He will not allow you to be put to shame. Discouragement comes to even the most valiant of men,

9

to the extent that some may consider suicide as a way out. But they that know who their God is, they who are certain that He is true and faithful, able and powerful to deliver, will hold on to God. Your God is with you and you are not alone.

He will strengthen you, He will help you, and He will uphold you. Be strong and courageous, God will be with you always. You can look to Him in the new year and be sure He will not fail you. You can hold on to Him all the days of your life and you will find Him to be true. Always!

Praying Points

Prayer: *Lord, thank You that You are leading and guiding me. I am so thankful that I have nothing to fear. In Jesus's name, amen.*

Prayer: *Lord, I recognize that You are the source of the life that I enjoy. Thank You for Your care and love toward me. In Jesus's name, amen.*

Prayer: *Lord, I can think of no better place to be than in Your hands. Now I take a moment and place my issues and concerns in Your hands also. In Jesus's name, amen.*

Prayer: *Lord, thank You for Your involvement in my life! Because of You, I can know deliverance, preservation, and restoration in my life. In Jesus's name, amen.*

Prayer: *Lord, I ask for Your leading and guidance in my life. Lead, guide, and direct me I pray, and show me which way to go. In Jesus's name, amen.*

Prayer: *Lord, thank You that You will never leave me or forsake me. Others may drop or abandon me but You will never let me go! In Jesus's name, amen.*

Prayer: *Lord, it is a great comfort and strength to know that You are with me. I am confident because my God is by my side. In Jesus's name, amen.*

Prayer: *Lord, I rejoice in the fact that You are for me. This gives me even greater confidence to trust You completely. In Jesus's name, amen.*

Prayer: *Lord, how thankful I am to know that You are with me! Because of this great fact I can be strong and filled with courage. In Jesus's name, amen.*

Prayer: *Lord, because You are with me, I have no reason to fear. In Jesus's name, amen.*

Chapter 2

WHY DO YOU NEED STRENGTH FROM GOD?

God Needs to Become Your Strength

And now, says the Lord—Who formed me from the womb to be His servant to bring Jacob back to Him and that Israel might be gathered to Him and not be swept away, for I am honorable in the eyes of the Lord and my God has become my strength.

—ISAIAH 49:5, AMP

EVERY ONE CREATED by God is for a specific divine purpose on earth. Each one is therefore valuable and precious to God. There is no accident with God and He is a God of purpose. If you do not matter in God's scheme of things, He would not have created you. Since He created you, you need to know then that you are of great value to Him.

Oftentimes we are derailed from our path by other people's attitudes toward us. We seek the approval of others so that we can feel good about ourselves. But many of those whose approval we seek have cruelly put us down, and we feel as if we have no value in ourselves. Know this: no matter what others have said, you are valuable.

For you to make your value count in this world, you need to cooperate with your maker. Go to Him and get from Him what your life was meant to accomplish. You have to trust that He will enable you to become what He has destined you to be. God is looking for those who will trust and obey Him.

So let God be your strength. There are moments that you feel like a reed drifting on water and life seems to hold no meaning. There are other times that the pressures of life can be overwhelming. Such times are mere indicators that you need more strength for life. Get up and go to God. God needs to become your strength.

DIVINE STRENGTH

> I can do all things through Christ who strengthens me.
>
> —PHILIPPIANS 4:13

Have you ever felt a need and did not know how to satisfy it? It can be really frustrating, can't it? You need to know you have access to God's storehouse of strength. God's strength is available to you!

You are a masterpiece of God's creation, but running on your own strength will bring you to exhaustion soon. The Creator designed you to renew your strength through Him.

Running on God's strength invigorates you! If you consider a tank of water that has a regular supply from a river, whatever that tank is meant to serve will be accomplished as long as the river keeps supplying the tank with water. So it is with receiving strength from God; you run the race of life without being weary.

When God strengthens you, you can handle anything. It is humility for man to know the extent of his capabilities, but the greater humility is in acknowledging that God can handle that incapacity. So it is not sufficient to just say that a task is beyond you; you have to go to God for strength to handle it. This is what Paul meant when he said he could do anything, because God gave him strength to do anything.

Trust God Always and Forever

> Trust in the LORD forever, For in YAH, the LORD, is everlasting strength.
>
> — ISAIAH 26:4

If you ever placed your trust in God at one point or the other in your life, then it is possible to trust Him all your life. Never stop trusting and having confidence in God. Trusting in God is not determined by specific circumstances; it is an attitude of the heart that is brought to play in all circumstances.

Hence, don't allow any situation, adversity, or trial to undermine your trust. The enemy would want you to label some circumstances as beyond the normal and thereby erode your confidence in God. But all situations, the ones you've called little and the ones you've seen as overwhelming, are the same, being incidents that occur in a man's life and require a solution. God gives solutions to all.

Trust Him, always and forever. In the little situations you should trust God, and in your overwhelming situations you should trust Him more. In fact, when a situation is overwhelming, that is when you need to trust Him more, for it is clear then that you alone were not meant to handle it!

The fear that man has in such troubling situations is that man's state of well-being or peace will be negatively affected. That is when you need to know that God is your eternal rock and your everlasting strength. As a rock, God will ensure your firm standing, immoveable in Him. This understanding gives strength to face the situation without fear of failure.

For When I Am Weak Then I Am Strong

> Therefore I take pleasure in infirmities, in reproaches, in necessities, in persecutions, in distresses for Christ's sake: for when I am weak, then am I strong.
>
> —2 Corinthians 12:10, kjv

It is a mystery of God's kingdom that the weak could declare his strength. Again, the understanding comes from knowing that you are not alone and that the situation which makes you feel helpless is not meant to be handled by you but by the God who is beside you. Paul had this understanding, and he could declare that it is in weakness that his strength is perfected because the divine strength, which is the ultimate in strength, is made available for him: For when I am weak, then I am strong.

If all you need is a solution, and solutions come from all kinds of intervention in a matter, you can rest on God, who is able to use anything and any situation to establish your joy. Consider this: if a situation becomes troubling to you, it is because at that moment and as far as you can see in the future, there is no help coming from anywhere. But imagine the next minute or hour or day, what you have not factored in to the matter happens and the situation takes a change. God comes through for His own people always.

Beyond giving you a solution when you are weak, God can even use you when you feel weak and powerless. It is interesting how someone who is bemoaning his woes suddenly finds himself becoming a vessel of comfort to another. God is surely beyond understanding! The story is told of a man who was facing bankruptcy and had to negotiate his debts at a bank. As he was about to enter the bank he met an orphan girl asking for alms. In his confused state of mind, he wondered if he shouldn't be begging too. He reached into his coat pocket to give something, only to find in that coat pocket a document he had been searching for, for many weeks—the document that would turn around his fortune.

Through their own situations, many have been able to give life-saving counsel unto others. The ways of God are past finding out. But in the time of adversity and trials, His strength makes you strong.

He Wants to Refresh the Tired and Weary

This is what the Lord Almighty says:

> "I will refresh the weary and satisfy the faint."
> —Jeremiah 31:25, niv

Do you feel tired, weary, and faint? Exhaustion is a feeling that comes when one has done all one could and the result is still not forthcoming. At such times the enthusiasm to continue with the task at hand is failing. In fact, one feels drained of all energy. Everyone comes to such a point at one time or another in life.

All manners of questions well up in the heart of the individual affected. There is the tendency to question one's ability or preparedness; sometimes one questions why such fate has befallen him or her. But whatever the myriad of questions in a man's heart, God has the answer.

God wants to refresh the tired and weary. As it was with Elijah in 1 Kings 19 after he defeated the worshippers of Baal on Mount Carmel and still had to flee from the threats of Jezebel, God brings refreshments. Elijah was so much in despair he said he was no better than his fathers, who had all failed in the matter, and he told God to kill him; but God knew all he needed was a new dose of strength. God gave him sleep and food and he was ready to go on.

God wants to strengthen you too. He gives strength to those who feel weak and faint, for He is not finished with you yet! You shall fulfill your destiny.

Be Strong and Of Good Courage

"Have I not commanded you? Be strong and of good courage; do not be afraid, nor be dismayed, for the Lord your God is with you wherever you go."
—Joshua 1:9

Everyone needs a form of booster to be able to pick up strength when one feels faint. There is no greater booster for the believer than the fact that God is with him. If the Source and Center of all things on earth is with you, you should be greatly encouraged.

But fear and doubt make us forget this fact of God's presence with us. The confrontations we receive from problems tend to mock us of unavoidable failure. We must deal ruthlessly with fear and doubt by affirming the divine presence all the time.

We must encourage ourselves to be bold and strong. Boldness and strength from God does not equal reckless bravado. No, it is the confidence in the unfailing Word of God which has assured us that God is with us! Sometimes the conviction you need of this divine presence may not be received until you have stepped into the situation. That's why you just must be bold.

Praying Points

Prayer: *Lord, I need You to come and strengthen me right now. Without Your strength I cannot cope, but with Your strength I can overcome! In Jesus's name, amen.*

Prayer: *Lord, You are the firm and unchangeable Rock on whom I can depend no matter what I may be facing. In Jesus's name, amen.*

Prayer *Lord, I need Your strength today! Come and empower me with Your divine strength. In Jesus's name, amen.*

Declaration: *God will honor those who make HIM their strength! I declare that God is my strength!*

Prayer: *Lord, I need the refreshing that only You can give. I need to be strengthened by You. In Jesus's name, amen.*

Prayer: *Lord, I will be bold and strong in the strength that You give me. In Jesus's name, amen.*

Chapter 3

GOD'S STRENGTH TO PRESERVE, PROTECT, AND DEFEND

The Lord Will Preserve You

Oh, bless our God, you peoples! And make the voice of His praise to be heard, Who keeps our soul among the living, And does not allow our feet to be moved.

—**PSALM 66:8–9**

IT IS WONDERFUL to know that God holds our lives in His hands. Therefore, nothing can happen to our lives without His knowing about it. The Bible often refers to His hands as the hands of strength, the hands that do valiantly. We can rest secure in those hands.

By holding you in His hands, God wants to preserve you. Preservation suggests an inherent threat to life, a tendency to extinction. But God wants you to feel His life in your heart, giving you a new spring of life and maintaining your own vitality.

When He preserves, imminent dangers are dispersed. He watches over you to ensure that you do not stumble or fall; your plans are upheld, your desires granted unto you. In such a state, you have the confidence that you will not be brought to adversity.

21

He also nourishes you with His provisions. God is known for changing the estate of man in a way that he can testify that he has been moved from a precarious situation into a state of well-being. God will bring you to a place of provision and blessing.

DIVINE PROTECTION

The LORD shall preserve you from all evil; He shall preserve your soul.

—PSALM 121:7

God is the protector and preserver of your life. In Ecclesiastes 9:12 the Bible says that the lot of man is like the lot of fishes caught in an evil net, when such a disaster falls suddenly. The fishes have lived all their lives in a river and simply expect that the place of life and fun will continue to be safe, but the evil net comes unawares and they are gone forever. In the same manner, man goes about his business in normal daily life, in the same community or business he has been used to all along, and does not expect any adversity to come upon him. Yet evil comes unannounced. Only God can be relied upon to preserve one from evil

Why should you rely on Him? First, He has walked through eternity future and nothing can spring a surprise on Him. Besides, He knows every route you take and can deliver you from a route that is dangerous while you may not see the immediate danger. That is why He is ultimately dependable to preserve your life.

Our help comes from God. In His own time and in His own way He shows up for us. The fact that we cannot fathom how He is going to show up has been our major unease. But it is sufficient that He will show up. We can remind ourselves of this fact, especially in difficult times.

You Will Not Stumble

> They shall come with weeping, and with supplications will I lead them: I will cause them to walk by the rivers of waters in a straight way, wherein they shall not stumble: for I am a father to Israel, and Ephraim is my firstborn.
>
> —Jeremiah 31:9, kjv

God has plans for each one of us. The One who made His plans for our lives is surely able to guide us into those plans. Moreover, He knows the path that will guarantee a smooth walk. You will not stumble!

The Bible says in Proverbs 19:21 that many are the devices of the heart of a man but the counsel of the Lord shall stand. Man makes his plans according to the limit of his understanding of things on Earth, but the understanding of God is infinite. Sometimes man does not know the connection between events in his life until the web shows a clear design. In hindsight he can then see the hands of God at work. His plans are always the best thing for us.

His plan is to bring you to a place of stability and clarity! You will be like one groping in the dark until you have an understanding that God is taking you to a sure destination. So, are you tossed to and fro in the tempest of this world? Let God be your anchor, and you can be sure that you are going to land on safe harbor.

Assurance of Divine Protection

He will not allow your foot to be moved; He who keeps you will not slumber.

—Psalm 121:3

The world is full of people who set their own desires above your good. These may want to see you stumble and fall so their desires can be met. It is the inherent nature in man to care for that which is his first, and when this care conflicts with another's, trust man to go to any length to remove the perceived obstacle notwithstanding what happens to you.

But God wants to see you standing strong without stumbling. Whatever others throw at you, God can ensure you are not moved by them. He made all things, and His purpose on Earth He can fulfill absolutely without bringing you into jeopardy.

He watches over you with great love and care. It is amazing how a little kid who has been given a pet hamster showers so much affection on that hamster. Should we not then trust our Father in heaven to care for us? His heart is tender toward us and He will not allow us to be moved.

Nothing escapes His view. Even the thoughts that are still being nursed in the mind are immediately available unto Him! Where a thing would end up is already known to Him. That is why He ensures that whichever way it goes you are still standing strong. He will hold you up.

THE LORD IS MY DEFENSE

> On the day when I faced disaster, they confronted
> me, but the LORD came to my defense.
> —PSALM 18:18, GW

We all face times or seasons of difficulty. As it happens to the affluent so it does to the poor. A man's challenge may take a different form from another's but everybody goes through it. It is wise therefore that after one has made all plans sure and sound that one still makes room for such difficult times.

When such times come, do not expect everyone to have sympathy for you. Some would consider you as deserving of what you are facing. Some would want to use your situation to justify their own challenges—he's not better than us after all! Many would rather face their own struggles than be concerned about yours.

But God is right in the midst of that situation with you. He never abandons or drops you. Because God came in the flesh, He has experienced all forms of struggles known to man and He is thus able to succor you. He will uphold you and keep you from falling.

God is your ultimate protector and guardian. David wrote in Psalm 66:8–9, "O bless our God, ye people, and make the voice of his praise to be heard: Which holdeth our soul in life, and suffereth not our feet to be moved" (KJV).

YOU ARE VALUABLE TO GOD

> Are not five sparrows sold for two copper coins?
> And not one of them is forgotten before God. But

> the very hairs of your head are all numbered. Do
> not fear therefore; you are of more value than
> many sparrows.
>
> —LUKE 12:6–7

Long before the knowledge of DNA and the complex structure of the body became more apparent, God already knew all the details of our lives. It was David who said in Psalm 139 that all the members of his body had been numbered by God even before he was born. The most minute detail is known to God as much as the interplay of these details in every organ of the body. The hairs of your head are numbered.

Numbering is not new to God. He numbered the stars in their trillions and knows where each of them is placed in the galaxy. So you can believe that the hairs of your head, which are far fewer than the stars, are no problem for Him. Nothing is hidden from His knowledge and nothing escapes Him.

You can believe therefore that He knows about the issues that you are facing. Whatever led to it He knows; whatever input that has come from various people and other factors He knows; whatever triggers your fear and anxiety in it He knows also.

But you do not need to fear, because you are valuable to God. If He watches over sparrows that are sold in the marketplace for insignificant amount, how much more will He watch over you whose soul is more valuable than all the treasures of this world to Him? In his understanding of the great value God has put in his life, David could pray in Psalm 17:8, "Keep me as the apple of Your eye; Hide me under the shadow of Your wings."

God Knows

> Then the Lord knows how to deliver the godly out of temptations and to reserve the unjust under punishment for the day of judgment. [Even good people face trials.]
>
> —2 Peter 2:9

Trials come to every man and you are not exempted. However it is every man that gives labels to his own trials; some label theirs impossible while some tag theirs insignificant. What label are you giving to yours? First Corinthians 10:13 tells us that every trial is common, not extraordinary as you might think. So your situation only seems impossible.

Yet, God knows how to deliver you. But we are not satisfied with the fact that He is going to deliver; we always want to know *how* God will do it! There are things in the realm of men, and that is why we are human, but that which is in the realm of the divine is of God and we should just leave the questions to Him. Let's trust Him.

God Will Undertake for You

> He will guard the feet of His saints, But the wicked shall be silent in darkness. "For by strength no man shall prevail."
>
> —1 Samuel 2:9

One feels such a grateful sense of relief and assurance when another stands with one in a cause. God will undertake for you. He recognizes the brethren of His dear Son Jesus, whom He has purchased by His own blood, and He takes their part in issues that concern them. They are the saints, made holy by the righteousness of Jesus who took their place on the cross where sin was judged.

God is therefore committed to watching over their moves. He will lead and guide you as you faithfully follow Him. The strength of man can never prevail because the factors of the supernatural are far stronger than what a man's natural strength can handle.

He will keep, protect, and defend you because you are His child and He loves you. As far as God is concerned, the wicked is the one who recognizes that his natural state tends to sin and evil and yet is unwilling to receive the redemption power of God through Christ Jesus. Essentially, such an individual is declaring that he is comfortable with sin and evil; that person has judged and condemned himself already. But the one who receives that power for a transformation of his life is honored by God with His protection.

The Hand of God Is a Saving Hand

Stretch out Your hand from above; Rescue me and deliver me out of great waters, From the hand of foreigners.

—Psalm 144:7

The psalmist David called for God to stretch out His hand from above to deliver. The hand of God is a hand of power and is able to do mighty things. David asked God to stretch His hand as a way of expressing the involvement of God in his matter. Just as a great warrior has power in his hand but that power is not accessed until the warrior is willing to be involved and thereby take action, the hand of God is a saving hand but God has to be implored to be involved in one's issues.

When that hand is stretched, however, be assured that it can reach and touch any situation. There are no limits as to what the hands of God can do; there are no failures or mistakes with Him either.

"Great Waters" are no challenge to Him. To the One who holds the world in His hands and who consider the world as a drop in the bucket (see Isa. 40:15), there are no great waters; only you have been overwhelmed by the situation.

All you have to do is to get Him engaged in your issue. Call on Him right now to stretch forth His hand. He shall deliver you and you shall be in peace.

Do Not Be Afraid

> Do not be afraid of sudden terror, Nor of trouble from the wicked when it comes; For the LORD will be your confidence, And will keep your foot from being caught.
>
> —PROVERBS 3:25–26

The term *unforeseen circumstances* has often been associated with an incident that comes suddenly upon an individual. While planners have used such circumstances to make allowance for contingencies in planning, the term, however, instills fear in some people. Do not be afraid of anything terrible that could come to you unawares.

It is tormenting for one to live one's life in fear. Fear establishes in an individual's heart the possibility of evil or wicked plans succeeding over one's life. But the Lord will be at your side and you will fear no evil.

Even when it is real that traps have been set, and all manners of devices have been contrived to bring you down, fear not still. God says in His Word in Proverbs 1:17 that it is in vain that one sets a trap in the eyes of the bird. Because God can see every device of the wicked against you, it is in vain that they set snares for your feet. God will be your protection and defense.

GOD WILL KEEP YOU

> This is what God the LORD says..."I, the LORD, have called you in righteousness; I will take hold of your hand. I will keep you."
> —ISAIAH 42:5–6, NIV

Just look what God says He will do: having called you, He promises to take hold of your hand and to keep you. Have you considered how secure a child is when he holds on to the hand of his father? That child draws strength and confidence from the father's grip, especially knowing that the father held on to him because he was pleased with him. In the same manner, God wants to have a walk with you and He calls you and holds your hand.

Do you recognize also the responsibility of God in this matter? Just as an adult who takes a child for a walk watches out for his safety on the roads and cares for his needs during the walk, God too has a responsibility to care for you.

God wants to preserve, maintain, defend, and watch over you. So let Him, by yielding to Him. If a child struggles to break free from the grip of the adult to burst loose on the roads, the adult surely sees to it that the child is brought under control because the adult knows the dangers on the road which are not known to the child. God will keep you; let yourself go in His hands.

HIDE ME IN YOUR PAVILION

> You shall hide them in the secret place of Your presence From the plots of man; You shall keep them secretly in a pavilion From the strife of tongues.
>
> —PSALM 31:20

Man is so full of schemes and devices. All manners of plots are hatched for the downfall of a man, but God's own scheme is to hide His beloved child from the consequences of such evil plots. Some of these plots are directed at maligning the character of an individual by speaking lies and all kinds of falsehoods and half-truths about him, trying to make him look dirty in the eyes of others.

The Bible says in James 3:6 that the tongue is a fire. What other people say can often affect us greatly. Precious relationships are jeopardized in the process, prospects are scuttled, and the heart is set in much pain, especially when such atrocities are carried out by those whom you trust. But God offers you a safe haven from the scourge of the tongue.

He wants to hide you in His pavilion. The idea of a pavilion is very interesting because God does not hide His beloved in a cell or cave but in a large place where liberty to operate is given unto His child. God's pavilion is a place of safety, a refuge from the hurt and evil intended for His child. Go to God, your refuge, and He will cover you with His wings.

David testifies in Psalm 121:5 that "The Lord is thy keeper: the Lord is thy shade upon thy right hand" (kjv). No one keeps better than God. He is so close that He is closer than your shadow. He is able to keep you to the very end.

The Lord Is Your Shield

The Lord is my Rock, my Fortress, and my Deliverer; my God, my keen and firm Strength in Whom I will trust and take refuge, my Shield, and the Horn of my salvation, my High Tower.

—Psalm 18:2, amp

He Is Your Rock

The Lord is my rock and my fortress and my deliverer; The God of my strength, in whom I will trust.

—2 Samuel 22:2–3

David wrote these after God had delivered him from his enemies. It takes one who has a firm assurance of who God is to pen these words. The battles of David were in no way trivial: he fought against a lion, a bear, and the giant Goliath. As if these were not daunting enough, the one who was to be his spiritual father and mentor chased him from cave to hold. But in all, God stood with him and gave him victory.

No matter how many, how persistent, and how disheartening your own battles may be, God wants to deliver you from your enemies too. What He did for a beloved of His in the past He will do for you now. The enemies of today may not be in the same guise as those of David, but whatever threatens your life, your peace and joy, is your enemy, and God will deliver you from them all.

He is your Rock, your Fortress, your Deliverer, and your Strength. Trust Him in everything and at all times.

On this Rock you can stand boldly. He is not a shaky ground or sinking sand but a solid Rock! The joy of salvation is that it brings a transition, indeed a translation, from a situation of despair and death unto life and glory. David said in Psalm 40:2 that "He brought me up also out of an horrible pit, out of the miry clay, and set my feet upon a rock, and established my goings" (KJV).

BE A SHIELD FOR ME

> But thou, O LORD, art a shield for me; my glory, and the lifter up of mine head.
> —PSALM 3:3, KJV

Why is God so interested in shielding you from the evil ones? First, His name and reputation are on your well-being. Besides, because you are such a precious vessel in preparation and He cannot afford to let the enemy waste you. God wants to be a shield around you.

God wants to lift up your head above all others. He is not only interested in lifting up your head when life gets too much and you drop your head; God wants to step into your life and lift up your head to be celebrated in the land of the living.

He wants to manifest His glory unto the world

through you. Who can have a better understanding of this than David? He was shielded by God from the bear and the lion when he was still tending sheep so he could be brought out against Goliath and for glory to shine forth on him. He was also shielded from the onslaught of Saul the king so that in his reign over Israel the glory of God could be seen through him, a glory so enduring that thousands of years after David is still being celebrated in Israel.

David also pleaded with God in Psalm 71:3, "Be my strong refuge, To which I may resort continually; You have given the commandment to save me, For You are my rock and my fortress." David does not want this refuge that has made him such a huge blessing to fail in his life. You too can call on God constantly to be your refuge.

MY HIDING PLACE

> You are my hiding place; You shall preserve me from trouble; You shall surround me with songs of deliverance.
>
> —PSALM 32:7

When God has hidden His beloved child from evil's way, it is not because God is weak. The hiding place is a place of recharge for the victories ahead. That is why the beloved of God is always surrounded with songs of deliverance. From one round of engagement in battles to another, the hiding place is an interlude and the songs of God's mighty works echo through the pavilion where the beloved child is hid.

Praying Points

Prayer: *Lord, I praise Your name and I trust You and what You are doing in my life. I know You hold my world in Your hands and You will preserve me. In Jesus's name, amen.*

Prayer: *Lord, I thank You that I can live securely knowing that You keep, preserve, and watch over my life. I commit this new week into Your hands. In Jesus's name, amen.*

Prayer: *Lord, in the complexity of life, with all its challenges and joys, I pray that You will hold me, so that I will not stumble, slip, or fall. In Jesus's name, amen.*

Prayer: *Lord, because You are with me, I have no reason to fear. In Jesus's name, amen.*

Prayer: *Lord, You are with me and this gives me the confidence to know that You will undertake in ALL matters that concern me. In Jesus's name, amen.*

Prayer: *Lord, You are my defense. You are my deliverer. You are my support. I look to You. In Jesus's name, amen.*

Prayer: *Lord, thank You that You love me and I am valuable and precious to You. In Jesus's name, amen.*

Prayer: *Lord, You are so faithful! You bring me through the tough seasons and help me so that I will not stumble or fall. In Jesus's name, amen.*

Prayer: *Lord, You know my situation. You know what I need and when I need it. I trust You with my life, knowing that You care for me. In Jesus's name, amen.*

Prayer: *Lord, You are the One who holds my future. You are my keeper and protector. I place my life into Your hands for today, and for the future. In Jesus's name, amen.*

Prayer: *Lord, You are great and You do great and wonderful things. Move in my situation I pray. In Jesus's name, amen.*

Prayer: *Lord, fill me with Your strength and give me the confidence to know that You will undertake and preserve and protect me. In Jesus's name, amen.*

Prayer: *Lord, as You call me, I respond and say "Yes." Take hold of my hand and keep me in all my ways. In Jesus's name, amen.*

Prayer: *Lord, I take refuge in You today. Hide me in Your pavilion and protect me from the strife of tongues. In Jesus's name, amen.*

Prayer: *Lord, I know that my life is safe in Your hands. You are my God and I will be confident in You! In Jesus's name, amen..*

Prayer: *Lord, I place my life safely into Your hands. Be my defender, my protector, and my shield. In Jesus's name, amen.*

Prayer: *Lord, I declare that You are my Rock, my Fortress, my Deliverer, and my Strength! In Jesus's name, amen.*

Prayer: *Lord, I place my life in Your hands today. Be my Rock and cause me to walk on solid ground. In Jesus's name, amen.*

Prayer: *Lord, it is a reassuring fact to know that You are with me and You will keep and guard me. I entrust my life into Your hands. In Jesus's name, amen.*

Prayer: *Lord, I pray that You will come and lift my head. I also pray that You will be a shield of protection around me. In Jesus's name, amen.*

Declaration: *God, You are my Rock of refuge and I will depend on You!*

Prayer: *Lord, be my Rock of refuge, be my Fortress, my Deliverer, and my Protector, I pray. In Jesus's name, amen.*

Prayer: *Lord, You are so faithful! You bring me through the tough seasons and help me so that I will not stumble or fall. In Jesus's name, amen.*

Prayer: *Lord, thank You that You are my hiding place from every storm that life may bring my way. You are my only security and I will trust You to keep and preserve my life. In Jesus's name, amen.*

Prayer: *Lord, hide me under the shadow of Your wings. Preserve me, guard me, and defend me I pray. In Jesus's name, amen.*

Chapter 4

REVIVING AND LIFTING UP OF THE SOUL

Awake!

*Wake up, sleeper, rise from the dead, and
Christ will shine on you.*

—**EPHESIANS 5:14, NIV**

O NE MYSTERY OF God to which every believer must subscribe is His newness every moment. Yes, He is the Ancient of Days, older than the oldest. Nevertheless, He is new every day. Besides being new every day, according to Isaiah 43:19, He does new things every day too. The revelation of God that anyone has yesterday is stale in itself because there is something new to learn about that God today.

He Himself declares in Revelation 21:5, "Behold, I make all things new." It's a new day, a new week, and a new opportunity for a new you. Every man is given a blessing of renewal but not all men take the chance of renewing themselves. While men groan on lost opportunities of yesterday and berate themselves on mistakes of the past, God is waiting for them to appropriate the new opportunities of today.

Believers must rise to the occasion and make the

most of it. There is a process of regeneration that is accomplished in us by the blood of Jesus. Furthermore, the Holy Spirit of God is the Spirit of renewal. Every day you should appropriate these blessings of renewal in your life. Rise from the ashes of failure and build anew. Leave behind the excuses of yesterday and take new steps for today.

As you do this, the very light of God will shine on you. God is at the center of this newness and He is willing to meet with the faith of whoever is ready to receive the blessings of it.

GOD WANTS TO LIFT YOU UP

> I waited patiently and expectantly for the Lord; and He...heard my cry. He drew me up out of a horrible pit [a pit of...destruction], out of the miry clay, and set my feet upon a rock, steadying my steps and establishing my goings.
> —PSALM 40:1–2, AMP

In life we can face great distress and trouble. According to Job 14:1, man that is born of a woman is of few days and full of trouble. Every man experiences things that bring them much discomfort, things that trouble their soul. But what to do at that time differs from man to man. The ultimate comfort for the believer is that the troubles will not drown him.

The trouble could so much overwhelm us that we sometimes feel we are buried deep within a pit. Like Joseph, we may feel hopeless like one cast into a pit without water. Other times, because of the many failed attempts to get a solution, we may even feel like we are stuck in miry clay.

It is true that we can face situations that we cannot get ourselves out of, but we are never beyond the reach of God. The move of God is beyond human comprehension. He comforts us by working out our release from such horrible pits. He rescued Joseph through his adversaries' desire for gain, and they sold him to slavery; unknown to those adversaries it was the first step toward fulfilling his dreams.

From the miry clay, He can pull you up and place your feet on a rock. That situation that draws you into hopelessness and utter despair is not beyond God. From slavery to prison, the situation of Joseph seemed to be getting worse, like one being drawn into miry clay. But the day God took him out and placed him on the seat of the prime minister of Egypt, his feet were placed upon solid rock! God will do for you in your own unique way the process of your lifting.

BE ENCOURAGED

> And David was greatly distressed; for the people spake of stoning him, because the soul of all the people was grieved, every man for his sons and for his daughters: but David encouraged himself in the LORD his God.
>
> —1 SAMUEL 30:6, KJV

In the midst of difficult times, David believed in his God. The desire of the enemy of your soul is for you to fail to recognize your ultimate ally in the time of trouble. When David and his men returned from battle to Ziklag and found their wives and children taken away and their homes burnt, they wept till they could weep no more;

a situation so hopeless that crack warriors broke down like babies.

While the enemy would come with all kinds of messages to cast down your heart into further despair, like the thought of whether your God is faithful in allowing such a terrible fate to be yours, God wants to revive your spirit with His power to do all things. David believed in this power and saw no need to weep anymore but sought the Lord as to the next line of action. You and I can do the same.

It is comforting when we have people around us who are people of good consolation. But sometimes we are alone. Worse, we may be the object of attack from others suffering the same fate as ours; our troubles therefore are multiplied! Nevertheless, we can remind ourselves of God's goodness and be encouraged. We can meditate on the good things we had received from Him in the past and be renewed in our trust in Him. We can consider the things around us that show us His faithfulness and be assured that He remains faithful still. Like David did, we should encourage ourselves in the Lord.

There is an end of everything. God's *modus operandi* ensures that the end is of good. According to Jeremiah 29:11, His thoughts toward us are thoughts of peace, and not of evil, to give us an already ordained end. Whatever happens, remember God is there and He will strengthen you.

THE LORD RENEWS MY SPIRIT

> Therefore we do not lose heart. Even though our
> outward man is perishing, yet the inward man is
> being renewed day by day.
>
> —2 CORINTHIANS 4:16

Besieged by all forms of trouble here in this world, our
bodies may feel tired but our spirits can be renewed.
We are human and the body is made by God to perish
one day; hence, weariness and tiredness may set in as
evidence of this perishing. But we are spirit beings.
Everyone that is born of the flesh is flesh and everyone
born of the Spirit is spirit. Therefore, the renewal of
our spirit is so important because it eventually revives
our body.

Because of this renewal of our spirit, we can overcome every discouragement. Discouragement comes
from the fear of our bodies perishing; from the fear of
harm to our bodies, the fear of lacking the resources to
care for our bodies. But when we have an understanding
that our spirit is the ultimate, we are not afraid of any
injury to the body; we are confident of the strength in
our spirit. Interestingly, the confidence in our spirit then
works upon our flesh to sustain the flesh and make the
fear disappear.

Therefore, you do not need to become discouraged.
Let God come and renew your spirit today. God is Spirit
and our relationship with Him is on the level of spirits.
The strength of your spirit is the extent to which you
make the best of your relationship with God. It is His
desire therefore to renew your spirit because He wants
you to have the best.

When your spirit is renewed by God you have reason to live. Your spirit will bubble with so much life that redefines your perception. The things that have made you feel hopeless suddenly take a new meaning, and you are able to see a tomorrow that is filled with joy and great expectations.

Lord, renew my spirit!

HE WILL SATISFY THE WEARY SOUL

> For I have satiated the weary soul, and I have replenished every sorrowful soul.
> —JEREMIAH 31:25

Have you considered marathoners on their course? They often pass by the water stands to take a swig. It is because they are given new strength in place of expended energy so they could continue the race to the end. Believers are on a course to heaven, and sometimes tiredness sets in and there is a need for a renewal. God wants to come and give strength to the tired souls.

God wants to replenish and satisfy each one of us. Just as it is the marathoners that make it to the finish line that are crowned, only the believers who make it to heaven are crowned. Because heaven is God's designed eternal home for us, He does not want us to give up on the way. Hence, He makes provision for us to be replenished on the way.

But just as no one forces the water on the marathoners but each one has to decide when to seek the replenishment, in the same manner, God invites us to come to His water stand and be replenished. If you feel faint or weary, come to Him, for He is here for you.

Sorrow has a way of draining away all the energy in a man. The physical exhaustion is the least of the damage sorrow brings; the emotional wreck it turns its victim into is far worse. Much more terrible than all these is the spiritual state of the victim that is impaired: the one in sorrow is in a state where he does not see a way out and it leads him to accept that there is no need to live any longer. But God brings such a person from the gloom unto the bright light of life through the refreshing that comes from the Holy Spirit.

LORD, FILL ME WITH YOUR LIVING WATER

"But whoever drinks of the water that I shall give him will never thirst. But the water that I shall give him will become in him a fountain of water springing up into everlasting life."

—JOHN 4:14

God has exactly what you need. The woman of Samaria at the well of Sychar had all kinds of desires: the desire for emotional comfort through a husband, the desire for acceptance in the society without the stigma of being a Samaritan or being a six-times-divorced woman. In the midst of all these desires, she saw the ultimate need of her life one day and those desires became irrelevant.

Though she was still a Samaritan six times divorced and without a husband, she found fulfillment in life. When God fills us, we are truly satisfied. The God essence is the Holy Spirit. The Holy Spirit brings a renewal and a refreshing that make other things insignificant.

That is why the Scriptures admonish us not to be drunk with wine but to be filled with the Holy Spirit

(Eph. 5:18). In the world today, people seek unto many things to feel satisfied. They become so confused in their seeking that they don't even know what it is they are seeking any longer, and they settle for a "high." Alcohol, drugs, sex, and all forms of things present themselves to these people as worthy of satisfying their heart desires. They are deceived into that which destroys life. Don't look to other things to give you fulfillment outside of the Holy Spirit

Look to God, He is the Source of every good and perfect gift. The ultimate end of God releasing Jesus unto the earth is for the release of the Holy Spirit. The Holy Spirit is all you need.

RECEIVE HIS STRENGTH AND PEACE RIGHT NOW

> The LORD will give strength unto his people; the LORD will bless his people with peace.
> —PSALM 29:11, KJV

God wants to strengthen you today. He is the Restorer of your strength. His strength is greatest when we are weak. So receive His strength and peace right now.

PRAYING POINTS

Prayer: *Lord, I shake off any negativity and defeat and I embrace the new things You have placed before me. Use my life and may my life reflect Your glory. In Jesus's name, amen.*

Prayer: *Lord, I receive Your strength right now. I will remind myself of Your goodness to* *me, no matter what happens. In Jesus's name, amen.*

Prayer: *Lord, lift me up out of those things that hold me down, and help me to stand secure on You, my firm rock and foundation. In Jesus's name, amen.*

Prayer: *Lord, I pray that You will come and renew my spirit right now. In Jesus's name, amen.*

Prayer: *Lord, restore my strength and fill me with Your peace I pray. In Jesus's name, amen.*

Prayer: *Lord, I need the refreshing that only You can give. I need to be strengthened by You. In Jesus's name, amen.*

Prayer: *Lord, come and refresh and satisfy me. Give me strength and enable me by Your Spirit. In Jesus's name, amen.*

Prayer: *Lord, fill me with Your living water and cause me to live a life that enjoys Your presence and blessing, each and every day. In Jesus's name, amen.*

Prayer: *Lord, renew me and renew my spirit, so that I can be invigorated and able to move ahead with what You have planned for me. In Jesus's name, amen.*

Chapter 5

POWER AND MIGHT

The Power of God Can Turn Impossibility to Possibility

*He turned the sea into dry land: they went through
the flood on foot: there did we rejoice in him.*

—PSALM 66:6, KJV

NOT ONLY WAS history made by the deliverance of a whole nation at the Red Sea, but also the incredible act of God was on display for the world to see. And fear came on all who heard about it: the God of Israel is mighty! Who can turn a sea into a dry land? None of their many gods could achieve that feat if they all came together as one. But because the Creator has the power to do as He wills with what He has created, God not only made the sea part and stand as walls on both sides for the children of Israel to pass, He also brought back the waters at the right time to drown all their adversaries!

God can turn impossibility into possibility. The reaction of the children of Israel at the beginning of the story showed that the situation was simply impossible; death stared down their faces. They stood at the bank of the Red Sea and could never figure a way of escape from the charging army of Pharaoh let alone see themselves at the other side of the Red Sea. But God is in the business of turning impossibilities to possibilities. All fears and anxieties are put to rest at the move of God's power and might.

Though the situation may be dreary, God always makes a way. The children of Israel did not need a diviner to tell them that the charging army of Pharaoh had no other intention than to destroy them, for the whole nation of Egypt was in sorrow by reason of the death of the firstborn of their men and cattle, and vengeance was in the air. Can you picture a situation in your life that is hopeless and at the same time life threatening as this?

God can turn a hopeless situation into a time of rejoicing. By the time the children of Israel got to the other side of the Red Sea and they saw enemies under whom they had been slaves for generations all buried in the Red Sea, their hearts burst into great rejoicing and shouts of deliverance; nothing other than celebration was appropriate in the circumstances. God can do the same for you and you will rejoice!

GOD IS THE GOD OF THE IMPOSSIBLE

> I will open rivers on the bare heights, and fountains in the midst of the valleys; I will make the wilderness a pool of water, and the dry land springs of water.
>
> —ISAIAH 41:18, AMP

The supernatural is always intriguing to man because man operates in the realm of the natural but God operates in the supernatural. Let's put it this way: the supernatural is the natural for God! God is the God of the impossible! Because man operates in the natural, oftentimes he transfers his natural qualities to God and then comes to a conclusion that God cannot do a thing about a situation either. But God is far more than what the heart of man can possibly understand.

God says, "I will..." and man wonders, "will He?" In the first instance, the means of hearing God is in the supernatural; natural eyes cannot see God, neither can natural ears hear Him. So an individual who receives a word from God must have stepped into the supernatural. How then can such an individual deny that the power that transcended the natural to bring about communication with God will fulfill the word that is spoken in that communication?

Are you in a valley or a wilderness, surrounded by foes, alone in the jungle of life, threatened by forces of darkness or lost in the wilderness of this world? There is a God who is the God of the impossible. He will sort you out. Even in your wilderness God can make pools of water, and your soul shall be refreshed.

Let expectation be alive in your heart. As Hebrews 11:6 says, he who comes to God must believe that God is, and He can do what he desires of Him. Your expectation shall not fail.

God can do the impossible. The impossible is reckoned by man as that which cannot happen following the natural sequence of things. But God transcends the natural. God can do the impossible. He can make a way in an impossible situation. He parted a sea to save a nation. He can make a way through your situation and save you.

MIRACLE WORKING GOD

My heart rejoices in the Lord! The Lord has made me strong. Now I have an answer for my enemies; I rejoice because you rescued me. [Hannah's prayer.]

—1 SAMUEL 2:1, NLT

At times, the situations of life come upon a man without negotiation. A man marries a woman and expects a child, but many years after, the marriage is still not producing a child. Doctors then come with a report that something in the man or woman cannot make a baby happen. But God can come through for you even in impossible situations.

Hannah was barren. Her husband had children through the other wife, so the problem was with Hannah. But God stepped into her situation and the woman that was called barren had the baby Samuel through God's intervention. Then joy filled her heart and she sang unto the Lord. You will also be able to rejoice because He will help you.

Celebrate the great things God has done for you. God does not need any encouragement through your worship because He cannot be "more God" than what He already is through your worship; He is perfect, the "I am that I am." But for you to receive from Him you need faith, and faith is stirred up through your worship. For in worshipping, you have the conviction that He can do for you what you desire.

When you believe God for the miracle, expect Him to answer and deliver you. Hannah sang of the deliverance of the Lord from shame and the reproach of her ene-mies. You will have an answer for your adversaries too.

Expect Your Miracle

And Joshua said unto the people, Sanctify your-selves: for to morrow the LORD will do wonders among you.

—JOSHUA 3:5, KJV

The air of expectation is a solid assurance of perfor-mance of miracles. Joshua prepared the hearts of the people for the wonders of God. You can imagine the people waking up the next day all waiting for the move of God. And God did move! We should always live with expectation.

Expect the Lord to do great things. He is the Lord over the heavens and the earth. All things are within His reach and are under His control; hence however great that thing you expect from Him, He will do it. So move your expectation higher to meet with the almightiness of God. Expect the Lord to perform miracles for you. Believe that He can, and expect that He will.

We serve a great and powerful God. All power belongs to Him. The forces in heaven, on earth, and underneath the earth all respond to His command. Nothing is beyond His command. He is greater in strength than all that could rise up against Him.

You are a child of God and He has employed all His strength and might to satisfy you. Like Joshua, you too should have an assurance that God is going to do won-ders in your situations. Never doubt or limit your great God. Those who trust in Him have nothing to fear.

PRAYING POINTS

Prayer: *Lord, You are my King, even over the floods of life that I may face. Help me to see the way of escape that You have provided, and let me soar with You above the storm. In Jesus's name, amen.*

Prayer: *Lord, You know the challenges I face. I pray that You will bring life into every area of my life. In Jesus's name, amen.*

Prayer: *Lord, I trust and believe that YOU will make a way for me. Bring me out on the other side, I pray. In Jesus's name, amen.*

Prayer: *Lord, You are great and You do great and wonderful things. Move in my situation I pray. In Jesus's name, amen.*

Our *Prayer for You: May you know His empowering strength today. In Jesus's name, amen.*

Prayer: *Lord, I take hold of Your hand right now. I need You to lead, guide, and hold me in life. In Jesus's name, amen.*

Prayer: *Lord, it is my longing and desire to know and enjoy the fact that You are with me and that Your hand is upon me. In Jesus's name, amen.*

Prayer: *Lord, those things that are impossibilities in my life I place in Your hands. You are the miracle-working God and I thank You for Your faithfulness to me. In Jesus's name, amen.*

Prayer: *Lord, be the strength of my life. Make me strong and may I enjoy Your presence in my daily life. In Jesus's name, amen.*

Prayer: *Lord, I believe that You can do great things, that You will perform miracles, and I live in expectation of the things You will do. In Jesus's name, amen.*

Prayer: *Lord, I declare that You are mighty. You are mightier than any situation or circumstance that I may face. In Jesus's name, amen.*

Chapter 6

GOD IS THE SOURCE OF STRENGTH AND SUPPORT

The Lord Is My Strength

Behold, God is my salvation, I will trust and not be afraid; "For YAH, the LORD, is my strength and song; He also has become my salvation."

—ISAIAH 12:2

For I am honorable in the eyes of the Lord and my God has become my strength.

—ISAIAH 49:5, AMP

Fear not, for I am with you. Do not be dismayed. I am your God. I will strengthen you; I will help you; I will uphold you with my victorious right hand.

—ISAIAH 41:10, TLB

THE PROPHET ISAIAH was the first prophet that God sent to guide the people of Israel with the word from the Lord, but the people always desired independence of God and would pursue the idolatrous ways of the nations around them. You can then picture the situation in which Isaiah found himself. But God always gave him strength to carry out his task. God wants to strengthen you.

At that time, Isaiah began to prophesy of the impending doom that the ways of the people would bring upon them. Without doubt he made enemies with such evil pronouncements and none was there to help him. God was his help and He wants to help you too.

When people in positions of power come against you, you feel vulnerable. You feel that they would oppress you with their positions and even do you harm. That was how Isaiah felt at that time too, but God upheld him. God wants to uphold you.

How does it feel for thousands of thousands to accuse you of treason, and you are alone in the position you have taken? It can be a really terrifying situation. None was willing to be on the side of Isaiah for his "strong words" against the people, but God supported him. God wants to give you support.

Isaiah prayed in Isaiah 33:2, "LORD, be gracious to us; we long for you. Be our strength every morning, our salvation in time of distress" (NIV). He pleaded for the grace of God to intervene in the moment of distress. Sometimes the situation can be so complex that all an individual needs is a daily relief. We are assured of God's strength every morning. His mercy, loving-kindness, and compassions are new every morning.

In the end, the people saw the truth in what Isaiah prophesied. They saw the judgment of God and came to a realization that they ought to have hearkened unto Isaiah. Then Isaiah was respected and promoted in the land. He even had the king request his counsel. God wants to lift you up and keep you elevated.

HE WILL STRENGTHEN YOU

> Yet the Lord is faithful, and He will strengthen
> [you] and set you on a firm foundation and guard
> you from the evil [one].
> —2 THESSALONIANS 3:3, AMP

God determines a thing He wants to do and then goes on to provide strength for His child so that he can withstand anything pertaining to that station. This is God's faithfulness at work, for He will not put His child in a place where he will be overrun by the adversaries. You can dare to believe that God wants to put you into a favorable position. It is a position of strength and security.

It can be frustrating to occupy a position and not have the ability to fulfill what is required at that position. That is why God strengthens His child to enable him to shine as a light in all his responsibilities. God's name is at stake in your life and in all that you do. Hence, He will strengthen you.

With the strength of God, you are set for the heights. But the one on that high pedestal often attracts detractors. Be not afraid; God is determined to guard you from the evil one. He is aware they may come up with plots to undermine your position and cause you to fail. But He will set you on a firm foundation; you shall not be moved. No activity against you shall be able to upset your life.

BE STRONG IN THE LORD

> Be strong in the Lord [be empowered through
> your union with Him]; draw your strength from

Him [that strength which His boundless might provides].

—Ephesians 6:10, amp

Empowerment is a word used in the Human Resources world to stress the need for one to be up to date in one's field and to develop the ability to perform excellently in that field. No child of God is allowed to be slothful; no child of God should be ordinary or average, because the strength of the Lord is available to build us up. Let God empower you.

You might have been moved to a new section of your operations and are feeling intimidated by the new challenges, but God is ready to give you His power and His strength. God is able to bring your way men and resources that will enhance your performance. When God told Moses to build the ark of the tabernacle, there was nothing like it ever built before. So God gave him the blueprint, but beyond that, God gave him Bezaleel, who had skill in working all manners of art to help him. And because God wanted Bezaleel to help Moses, even Bezaleel was given strength by God to do so.

But this strength from God happens as we stay connected with Him. It's like a power grid that does not flow to the disconnected. When you take off the power cord of your refrigerator or television, energy is cut off. But that does not mean energy is not available in the house; only those items disconnected would not have energy. Though the power of God is unceasing, you have to stay connected to God to benefit from that unceasing source of power and energy.

When you have received the strength, stir yourself up and prove yourself able in the Lord. It is written in the Book of Judges that Samson would stir himself up whenever the power of God came upon him, and he was able to do mighty things. Be strong with the Lord's mighty power.

We need to be strong as we face the responsibilities of each day. Each day has its own challenges. Even a task that we have been performing for a long while may take a new turn on a particular day and leave us at a loss as to how to handle it. But we need to be strong and convince ourselves that we can do it by the help of the Lord.

Moreover, we need strength as we face the future. The uncertainty of the future is always a bother to many. We wonder if we would maintain our position or if market trends or new technology will overwhelm us. But we must believe that the Lord who has given strength to make us what we are today will still be there for us tomorrow.

The strength of the Lord is not a feeling or a force of nature; He is a person. Who is this Strength of the Lord? He is the Holy Spirit, and you should let the power of the Holy Spirit strengthen you. He is the Spirit from the beginning of creation who moved to bring to existence the heavens and the earth. You can do things in His strength.

The Lord Is My Support

> They came upon me in the day of my calamity, but the Lord was my stay.
> —2 Samuel 22:19, amp

It is enough woes when calamity befalls an individual. But the taunts of men and the mischief of trouble-makers add pepper to the injury. Even some wicked people come to finish up the individual so that he will never rise again. Only the Lord can deliver at such times.

Trouble comes uninvited and without notice. It can come on us in our weakest and lowest moments, making us unprepared to fight back. At such times, we feel vulnerable and want to collapse under the heavy burdens. But God knows our weakness and would not allow anything beyond our strength to overcome us. So He steps in to bear us in His hands and steady us.

God knows the tactics of the enemy. The enemy wants to rush at us and cast us down. But as the Word of God assures us, when the enemy comes in as a flood, the Spirit of the Lord would raise a banner against the onslaught of the enemy (Isa. 59:19). We can be sure that God is there holding us up in the face of challenge and adversity.

The Lord Is My Immovable Rock

> The Lord...is my immovable Rock. He gives me strength.
>
> —Psalm 144:1, TLB

Most things in life are not *sure* things! A system may favor you today and by tomorrow your position in the system may be missing. Help may arise from a quarter today and the next day, that quarter may close all doors. The hymn writer Edward Mote writes, "On Christ the solid Rock I stand; all other ground is sinking sand."[1] No ground is dependable in this world.

---

1   Edward Mote, "My Hope Is Built on Nothing Less," 1834. Public domain.

That is why we need a sure foundation. Jesus is that immovable Rock. When all the world structures and systems have dealt with you, you can still be secure on this firm foundation. God is like the reassurance in any insurance venture. Knowing you can fall back on Him in security gives you strength.

Everything in life begins somewhere and we call it the foundation. A house is built on a foundation just as a career is built on a foundation. The education of a child is a foundation for life; a seminary is a foundation for ministry. If we have a good foundation in any area of our endeavor we will be strong. Yet God is the foundation that holds all endeavors in life together. Make God your foundation and be strong!

TURN TO GOD FOR STRENGTH

> Now David was greatly distressed, for the people spoke of stoning him, because the soul of all the people was grieved, every man for his sons and his daughters. But David strengthened himself in the LORD his God.
>
> —1 SAMUEL 30:6

There is so much in life that can get us distressed and concerned. Family issues, business ventures, and health matters can put us in distress. The weight of the distress is heavier when you bear other people's distress as well.

David was honored and celebrated as a valiant man, the giant slayer. He was the toast of the king and the leader of the warriors. But he found himself "greatly distressed" at times! So even the most valiant is brought to his knees sometimes.

The question, however, is, Whom do we turn to in times of distress? Most of us turn to men. The very men who had showed loyalty and support to David all along now turned against him. They heaped the weight of their distress on David and even thought of stoning him to death.

We must always turn to God and find our strength in Him. Not only is it impossible for God to be distressed, it is also impossible for Him to withdraw from giving help, or to fail

Praying Points

Prayer: *Lord, I believe, beyond a shadow of a doubt, that I can trust You completely. You are my God and the strength of my life. In Jesus's name, amen.*

Prayer: *Lord, I receive everything that You have for me today. I declare that I can do ALL things through Christ who strengthens me. In Jesus's name, amen.*

Prayer: *Lord, You are my protector, my provider, my strength and my security. You are MY faithful God. In Jesus's name, amen.*

Prayer: *Lord, I receive Your strength right now. I take hold of Your hand and I am strengthened now. In Jesus's name, amen.*

Declaration: *I can do all things through Christ who strengthens me!*

Prayer: *Lord, as I start this new day and this new week, I ask You to strengthen me and to give me the courage I need. In Jesus's name, amen.*

Declaration: *God is my Rock—I will not be moved and HE will strengthen me!*

Prayer: *Lord, hold me up, I pray. Be my support and protect me, I pray. In Jesus's name, amen.*

Prayer: *Lord, I turn to You. I look to You and I find my strength in You. In Jesus's name, amen.*

Prayer: *Lord, I need Your strength today! Come and empower me with Your divine strength. In Jesus's name, amen.*

Declaration: *God will honor those who make Him their strength! I declare that God is my strength!*

Chapter 7

GOD CAN!

God Can Do Exceedingly Abundantly Above All

*[He] is able to do exceeding abundantly
above all that we ask or think.*

—Ephesians 3:20

W HEN YOU APPROACH God, you are approaching
your Provider: He gave you life in the first instance.
The One who gave life can give all that life needs.
The needs of a man are perceived in the light of that
man's circumstances and his assessment of people and
systems around him, but God knows what a man truly
needs.

The man at the gate called beautiful thought his need
was mere alms from the people. So when Peter and
James came to him, he asked them of alms. You could
then imagine the disappointment that welled up in him
as he heard the first words of Peter, "silver and gold we
have none..." (Acts 3:6). He must have thought that an
encounter with them would not meet his needs that day.

But the Lord, who can do exceeding abundantly above
all that we ask or think, had a great surprise waiting for
him. What he never bargained for was given to him. His

real need was to overcome his lameness and have the use of his feet so he could walk and fend for himself, but seeing no way how such could happen, he considered his need to be alms offered by people for his sustenance.

That the Lord can do exceeding abundantly above all means that He can do things to an extent we cannot expect and beyond what words can express. God's deeds always fall in the realm of the astonishing and the incredible, because He is God. Don't doubt God, just ask Him and expect Him to move.

The power that fulfills all things is the Holy Spirit, and that power is at work in our lives by the reason of the name of Jesus which we bear. You can believe that God will exceed your expectations.

God Is Able to Make You Fruitful

And the second he called Ephraim [to be fruitful],
For [he said] God has caused me to be fruitful in
the land of my affliction.
—Genesis 41:52, amp

When God created man, His command to man was for man to be fruitful (Gen. 1:28). There is a quality of fruitfulness God programmed into the masterpiece He created called man. It was such a significant quality with God that when the earth was wiped away during the Flood and God began again with Noah, His command to Noah was to be fruitful (Gen. 9:1).

Even in circumstances prone to stifling fruitfulness, in circumstances of affliction, God still makes His own children fruitful. The children of Israel were in slavery for centuries but in the midst of such suffering, the

Bible records that they were so fruitful and multiplied that they filled the land to the extent that Pharaoh had to order the death of little babies to stop the process of multiplication.

God's interest in the fruitfulness of a people begins with the fruitfulness of individuals. Joseph suffered afflictions in the land of Egypt where he was sold to slavery by his brothers. From slavery to prison, his ordeal grew worse. Yet the Lord brought him forth one day to occupy the exalted position of the prime minister of Egypt. God is able to make you fruitful regardless of your situation or circumstances.

In bondage as a slave and a prisoner Joseph was still fruitful, even in a foreign land. You can be fruitful, abundantly productive in your situation. There is a quality of God in you, a seed of fruitfulness, which will answer to the call of God for you to be fruitful. Give God your situation, and expect to be fruitful.

God Can Turn a Wilderness into a Fruitful Field

> Is it not yet a very little while Till Lebanon shall be turned into a fruitful field, And the fruitful field be esteemed as a forest?
>
> —Isaiah 29:17

The desert is a barren ground, largely because of the scorching heat that dries up life from any plant there and also because of the lack of water and moisture. The land in the desert is sandy and cannot support growth of plants. Yet God in His power says He can turn a desert into a fruitful field. Yes, He can!

There are situations in the life of a man that are

comparable to a desert. When a man is not productive and every business or venture he goes into collapses and dies, the land of such a man is like a desert. When the conditions that should produce a child in the womb of a woman are absent, such a womb is called barren. But God can turn all these situations around into great fruitfulness. Yes, He can!

Desert experiences are a part of life. One must know, however, that God is not interested in making the situation remain so. God can turn a wilderness into a fruitful field. Give God those barren areas of your life and He will transform them.

God Is Able to Deliver You

David said, The Lord Who delivered me out of the paw of the lion and out of the paw of the bear, He will deliver me out of the hand of this Philistine.
—1 Samuel 17:37, amp

Have you ever come into a situation so strait that you cannot see a way out? That is the typical ground for God's deliverance. Imagine David tending to his sheep and a lion comes out of nowhere against him and his few sheep to destroy them. It takes strength from God for deliverance to take place that day. God is able to deliver you from whatever it is that you are facing.

When deliverance occurs, the faith of an individual is strengthened and he can believe God for deliverance in other circumstances. This was the testimony of David when he came against Goliath. While everyone else bolted into caves and holes at the sight of Goliath, David remembered the deliverance he received from the lion and the bear, and he was confident that the same God would deliver him from Goliath. As far as he was concerned, all these adversaries wanted death for him, but God had preserved his life for His glory and so none of them could take it away.

God brought you through the trials of the past and He will continue to rescue you. Would He deliver you from the evil of the past only to release you into the evil of today? Definitely not, or else He might as well have allowed you to be destroyed the other times. Don't doubt His power and ability in your life. He will deal with the "giants" that would try to destroy you!

GOD WILL SEE YOU THROUGH

> No weapon that is formed against you shall prosper.
> —ISAIAH 54:17, AMP

Weapons are instruments of war and wars are fought to destroy lives. Your life is, however, so precious in the hands of God that He will not allow it to be destroyed. God was giving the prophet Isaiah a measure of confidence here, declaring unto him that He made the very person who designs weapons of war and He fashioned the evil that was intended to be accomplished through the weapons of war, but that neither the design of the weapon nor the intended evil had you as the targeted end.

God identifies here that the weapons could be allowed to come into existence. The implication here should not be lost on us: the evil ones could bring up their forms of attack. But God assures us that however carefully crafted or potentially deadly the weapons of the enemies may be, He will not allow it to prosper over our lives.

As people of God, we have a God who fights for us in diverse ways when we face attacks. Sometimes He arises to destroy the enemies; some other times He allows the enemies to go to great lengths in bringing up their weapons of attack and He goes on to frustrate the weapons from functioning. Whichever way He chooses to give you the victory, all you know is that you will be delivered.

God will see you through. God is greater than anything you may be facing! Hence, be assured that you will not be hurt or put to shame in the battles of life. You will prevail.

Opportunities Do Not Last Forever

I must work the works of him that sent me, while
it is day: the night cometh, when no man can work.
—John 9:4, kjv

In the bid to prosper His people, God brings opportunities across their way. These opportunities are, however, time specific. There is a measure of serious work and attention that God expects to be given to the opportunities He has created for you.

Jesus Christ, who was God in the flesh, declared that there is a day and night situation attached to tasks and opportunities. The day is the time to work and the night is the time to cease from working; the day is the time to explore the opportunities and the night is the time to rest. The reference to the day here does not necessarily mean twenty-four hours; rather it depicts a time frame, a period when the execution of a task is profitable.

Each day, each period, is another opportunity to do what God wants us to do. The lifetime of an individual is measured in batches of opportunities, but opportunities do not last forever. Someone once said that opportunity is like a fair woman—good looking and promising, and with a lot of hair on her head; and if someone decides to let her pass by thinking there would still be hair to grab at the back of her head, that person will discover too late that the woman is bald at the back of her head.

Look out for opportunities and don't let them slip by. It is a great disservice to the God who created the opportunities for you to trifle with them. Make the most of every situation and circumstance.

I Can Do All Things Through Christ

> Finally, my brethren, be strong in the Lord and in the power of His might.
> —Ephesians 6:10

When God has created the enabling circumstances for success, there is still one very important factor that makes the success happen, and that is you. Your attitude toward the situation that confronts you is a decider in the overall.

People have attained success in life in spite of incredible situations of lack and suffering. These success stories always show a belief in the person's ability to pull through the situation. Many had attempted several times to achieve a particular result and failed but persisted because something in them kept on reassuring that they would break through.

Paul put the source of his own strength in Christ. The encouragement he received daily was from knowing that Christ has settled all that pertained unto his destiny. Everyone needs strength to pull through difficult circumstances. We need to be strong as we face today. We need strength as we face the future. Who will be your strength reviver?

Let the power of the Holy Spirit strengthen you. The Holy Spirit is the Strengthener that Jesus Christ has provided for His people. With Him, you can do all things and nothing shall be impossible for you.

God Has Many Plans for You

He [God] is unchangeable...what He wants to do, that He does. For He performs [that which He has] planned for me, and of many such matters He is mindful.

—Job 23:13–14, AMP

God does not change like the weather. He is consistently the same, doing what He said He would do. Why do people go back from doing what they promised to do? Sometimes what they said they would do was not well thought out before they said so. Oftentimes they are serious about doing it but they lack the resources to make good on their promise. But God does not only have all the resources of heaven and earth to fulfill His promises, He also has the ability to make it happen. Besides, the One who dwells in eternity past and eternity future has a total, global picture of things and cannot err in thought or deed.

Job, in the midst of afflictions, still recognized this ability of God. Of course, He was testifying to the riches and abundant prosperity he received from God earlier in his life. He was so wealthy that he was the greatest in the entire East, and he submitted that it was God fulfilling the plans He had for him that was the secret of his success.

One interesting element of God's ability to perform His promises is that no one can resist Him. Once He decides to do a thing, no one can say anything to the contrary. He has all the forces of heaven and earth subject to His command and He discharges them to anyone and any situation where He wants to be involved. He wants to be involved in the affairs of your life.

God has many plans for you too. Before He set your feet on planet Earth, He ordained a destination for you. He controls your destiny. He will fulfill them all and your joy shall be full.

GOD KNOWS ALL THINGS

You saw me before I was born and scheduled each day of my life before I began to breathe.
—PSALM 139:16, TLB

It is often said that knowledge is power. The more an individual knows about a project or system, the more the ability to perform in that project or system. To be relevant in an organization or society, the knowledge of the operations of that organization or society is crucial.

It is wonderful to know that God knows all things. Even before the creation of anything on Earth, God already knew what that thing would look like. That is why when He saw each aspect of creation He could say that it was good, conforming to blueprint. Also, God already knows what will be at the end of time. That is why He could take John the beloved to heaven in the Book of Revelation and show him things to come.

In the life of a man, too, the knowledge of God about what the life holds is endless. David's confession of the awesomeness of God's knowledge is inspiring. David said that God knew the various parts of his body even before those parts were put together in his mother's womb. He further said those parts were numbered by God and He knows the sum of them all.

From eternity past to eternity future, God knows all things, and without doubt He knows today. Today is a gift that God has given you. Everything about this day He already knows. And if He knows, then He already knows how it will all play out. No matter what you are facing you can trust that God knows about it specifically and He knows how it will play out. Since He said His thoughts toward you are thoughts of good and not of evil, be confident that the day shall turn out for good.

God Can Turn Any Situation Around

And they kept the Feast of Unleavened Bread seven days with joy; for the LORD made them joyful, and turned the heart of the king of Assyria toward

them, to strengthen their hands in the work of the
house of God, the God of Israel.

—EZRA 6:22

When friends arise to help you, there is nothing unusual
about that, but when enemies work out your good with
zeal, surely there is an element of the unexpected in it.
When an idolatrous king ordered the construction of
the house of the God of Israel, the people of Israel could
not believe their ears. God not only strengthened the
hands of King Cyrus of Persia but guided him to fulfill
the desire of His people, Israel.

This scenario would get more interesting still. The
king and people of Assyria in the history of the children of Israel were sworn enemies of God's people. But
in the time of Ezra, the unexpected took place: God
made the king of Assyria help to reinforce the order of
Cyrus that the construction of the house of the God of
Israel might happen!

God can turn any situation around. The problem with
men is that they have boxed God into their finite calcu-
lations as if to say to God that He cannot pass the limit
of their thinking. What may seem unlikely and impossible God can change. God changed the heart of a king,
and he became favorable toward God's people.

Who could ever believe that Moses, who escaped
the sword of the king of Egypt in his days, would turn
out to be nursed by the daughter of that Pharaoh? The
one that was caught in the decree of death at his birth
ended up being raised in the palace of the one who
issued the decree. To add to the beauty of the situation, the mother who with a heavy heart had to let go
of her baby at the banks of the Nile and who thought

that death had eventually caught up with her son was the one that was called upon to nurse the child and to get paid for that labor!

In the same manner of God's omniscience and omnipotence there is a record of the explosion of the population of the people of Israel in Exodus 1:12. It is written that the more the Egyptians afflicted them, the more they multiplied and grew. And their afflicters were in dread of the children of Israel. This is clearly against the natural order of things. One would have thought that afflictions would deplete the people, but the contrary was the case. Someone joked that what probably happened was that the sufferings brought unto the people the need for comfort they could only get from their spouses, and the result was babies being turned out rapidly. But the fact of the case was that a people under oppression became a threat to their oppressors.

Times of difficulty can often be times of growth. How does one explain the growth of the cactus in the desert? It is said that those adverse desert conditions were the springboard for the plant that not only survives the heat and dryness of the desert but also has the most liquid in the desert. It reminds one of the story of little boys who went to pick fruits at an orchard. Though they were forbidden to do so, they took a long route to walk around the high fence of the orchard and to creep in at a small opening under the fence. But when the owner of the orchard saw them at a long distance, he released his fierce dogs after them. At seeing these dogs, the children did a sprint that would probably break the records for kids of their age. As they ran for their lives they saw the high fence as an obstacle in front of them, but seeing the fierce dogs behind them, they didn't think twice before attempting to scale the fence; all of them accomplished that feat they had initially thought was impossible.

Does God put some obstacles in front of His child to get that child to know the abilities He has deposited in him? Times of challenges can often be times of multiplication. Muscles are built in the process of exertion. The resistance that comes against a sportsman actually builds him up to overcome that resistance and any other which come up in future.

In the same manner, God can take what was intended for evil and turn it around for good. The story of Joseph is a classic example. His own brothers plotted to kill him but changed their minds and sold him into slavery. As far as the brothers were concerned that was good riddance to bad rubbish. Unknown to them, they had just pushed him to where God needed him to fulfill his greatness. Joseph ascended to a throne where he was not only honored in that foreign land with the highest title second only to the king, but was also put in charge of the administration of resources for the entire world at that time. By then, Joseph himself told his brothers that what they meant for evil God had turned around for good for him, their family, for Egypt, and for the whole world.

Let God use your situation to bring about His plans and purposes. Let God work in your situation and He will cause things to change. He cannot be boxed by your limited understanding of things.

NOTHING IS TOO HARD FOR GOD

> God can do anything, you know —far more than
> you could ever imagine or guess or request in
> your wildest dreams! He does it not by pushing us
> around but by working within us, his Spirit deeply
> and gently within us.
>
> —EPHESIANS 3:20, THE MESSAGE

The way of God is unsearchable. As the wind that blows and one knows not where it comes from and where it is going but the impact is seen eventually where it passes, so is it with God. God is at work in each of our lives. Perhaps the problem with man is that he wants to hear a great noise and see things tumbling for him to accept that God is at work. But as Elijah would discover when he presented himself before God in 1 Kings 19:12, God was not in the earthquake, neither was He in the whirlwind or the fire, but there He was in the still small voice! The man who called fire from heaven thought that God could only be present in the violent actions and could not understand why God was "hesitant" in destroying Jezebel, the priestess of Baal, along with her fellows.

God works in a gentle way, without pushing and shoving. When He comes against the workers of iniquity to destroy them, it is to resist evil on Earth. And the perpetrators of evil would have been given a long rope to pull before they sealed their fate with stubbornness and irreverence to God. But as for the child of God, he must understand the quiet ways of God at work. Yet we always desire to see signs, which in themselves are evidences of our unbelief.

We must not forget that God can do anything! More

than our minds can project, more than our perceptions of the situation. A child looking at a truck sees a massive thing impossible to handle, but his father the truck driver sees a vehicle that yields to his control. What may look like a mountain to you is not a mountain to God!

God declares in Jeremiah 32:27 that He is the God of all flesh and that there is nothing too hard for Him. If He made all flesh on Earth and He is in control of all of it, surely He can move all men to do His will. He will move them to fulfill your life.

ENABLE ME, O GOD

> In the day when I called, You answered me; and You strengthened me with strength (might and inflexibility to temptation) in my inner self.
> —PSALM 138:3, AMP

There is a blessing in store for those who trust the Lord. The one who believes in all the ability and power of God receives the blessings from them. David trusted in the Lord and was always calling on Him for his rescue and deliverance. Each time, God showed up for him.

Trusting God leads to life. Many of the horrible crimes committed on Earth are done by people who have no hope of life, who see no more good in themselves. But the one who places his trust in God always has the hope that God will answer him when he calls on Him. This is what John wrote in 1 John 5:15, that we have an assurance that we have our petitions which we ask of Him when we are sure that He has heard us.

Ask God to enable you to accomplish things. Don't give up. Ask Him to work on your behalf. David said in

Psalm 57:2 (AMP), "I will cry to God Most High, Who performs on my behalf and rewards me [Who brings to pass His purposes for me and surely completes them]!" When you call on Him, He will bring to pass His purposes for your life. He will complete the good work He started by creating you and bringing you to your present state of being.

Depend on God to bring you through whatever you are facing. Make the Lord your hope, and He will establish you.

PRAYING POINTS

> **Prayer:** *Lord, I am so glad that You want to strengthen me. Come and strengthen me right now so that I will be able to do ALL things because of Your strength. In Jesus's name, amen.*

> **Prayer:** *Lord, I appreciate the fact that You are at work in my life. Help me to always do what pleases You. In Jesus's name, amen.*

> **Prayer:** *Lord, You know my situation. Help me to make the best use of what You have given me and where You have placed me. Cause me to be fruitful and productive. In Jesus's name, amen.*

> **Prayer:** *Lord, I give You those areas of my life which are barren and unproductive. Please transform those areas of my life into areas*

that are fruitful and fertile. In Jesus's name, amen.

Prayer: *Lord, I know that You are able and will deliver me from my enemies. You have been faithful in the past and I know that You will continue to be faithful. In Jesus's name, amen.*

Prayer: *Lord, You are my King and I bring to You all my requests, knowing that You are able and will do even more than I could have asked or imagined. In Jesus's name, amen.*

Prayer: *Lord, I trust and believe that YOU will make a way for me. Bring me out on the other side, I pray. In Jesus's name, amen.*

Prayer: *Lord, You are my great God and You will see me through! In Jesus's name, amen.*

Our *Prayer for You: We pray right now for all those reading this prayer. Lord, we pray that You will come and strengthen and aid them, because they need Your empowering strength. In Jesus's name, amen.*

Prayer: *Lord, open my eyes to see the things that You have pre-prepared for me. Give me the courage to take advantage of the opportunities I have. In Jesus's name, amen.*

Declaration: *I can do all things through Christ who strengthens me!*

Prayer: *Lord, You are God and my life is in Your hands. Fulfill Your purposes in my life and bring Your plans for my life to pass. In Jesus's name, amen.*

Prayer: *Lord, today is another day that You have given to me as a gift. I rejoice in the fact that You know all things and especially the things that I am facing today. In Jesus's name, amen.*

Prayer: *Lord, I know that You are able to change the different aspects of my situation and to cause things to work in my favor. I give You my circumstances and I ask You to work things out. In Jesus's name, amen.*

Prayer: *Lord, You know every aspect of what I am facing. I place it all in Your hands knowing that You can take an oppressive and difficult situation and make it work for my good! In Jesus's name, amen.*

Prayer: *Lord, I am so thankful to know that nothing is too hard for You! Thank You for the work You are doing in my life. Continue to work in my life in Your own gentle way, I pray. In Jesus's name, amen.*

Prayer: *Lord, You are my King, even over the floods of life that I may face. Help me to see the way of escape that You have provided, and let me soar with You above the storm. In Jesus's name, amen.*

Prayer: *Lord, You are my hope! The power of Your strength in me enables me. In Jesus's name, amen.*

Prayer: *Lord, I am so glad that You want to strengthen me. Come and strengthen me right now so that I will be able to do ALL things because of Your strength. In Jesus's name, amen.*

Prayer: *Lord, I call on You to bring to pass the things You have promised me. Work on my behalf and do something wonderful! In Jesus's name, amen.*

Chapter 8

STRENGTHENED BY HIS GUIDANCE

God's Hand Is There for You

*Even there shall Your hand lead me, and
Your right hand shall hold me.*

—PSALM 139:10

CAVE EXPLORERS HAVE learned the age-long lesson of seeking a guide familiar with the environment of the cave they want to explore. Somehow they know that the guide would be familiar with routes they had not taken before, and they know that the guide knows about potential dangers from animals and other dwellers in and around the cave. Man comes to planet Earth not knowing much about what the Earth is about and how things function on Earth, but with arrogance neglects the help of a guide. But the one who seeks unto God as his Guide does not make a wreck of his life but gets to the end of his journey.

Life is not always easy. We don't get things at the snap of a finger; oftentimes it's a lot of hard work and struggles to get a thing done. Besides, things don't come to us as we have planned them. Things don't always turn out as we had hoped. The variables in the affairs of life cannot be absolutely programmed for the desired results. This is the wisdom of seeking the Guide who will help us navigate the uncertain terrains.

God has a way of working things out. God's hand is there for you! Reach out and take hold of His hand!

Ezra the scribe has this testimony in Ezra 7:28: "I was strengthened and encouraged, for the hand of the Lord my God was upon me" (AMP). The good hand of God holds His child and ensures that the child does not miss his way. Also, the good hand assures the child of strength to confront the situations in his life. In our lives, especially in tempestuous times, we can experience the hand of God. That hand will hold us and lift us up.

DIVINE GUIDANCE

> The LORD will guide you continually, And satisfy your soul in drought, And strengthen your bones; You shall be like a watered garden, And like a spring of water, whose waters do not fail.
> —ISAIAH 58:11

The Lord wants to guide you on an ongoing basis. It is often the case that when man has gone his own way, after the limit of his own knowledge, and has found himself to be completely lost, that is when he begins to look for a guide. But at such times, it is usually too late to find one. God is willing to guide you continually if you will always bring yourself to Him. Even if you found out that you have missed the mark a long way, with God it is never too late to seek for guidance as long as you still have your breath in you.

With the guidance of God comes a guarantee of

arriving at a safe haven, a destination of great well-being. He will lead you to a place where He can satisfy you, even in drought conditions. This is true because drought conditions arise from the displeasure of God upon a land. Surely He would know the land where His displeasure is manifesting and guide you away from there. And if He chooses to take you into that land as He took Joseph to Egypt, He will turn around the lot of the people of that land because of you.

Drought dries up the bones. Pictures of children in nations or communities stricken by drought are usually pitiable. Swollen heads and tummies resulting from kwashiorkor, all manners of diseases riding on the back of that leanness, cause a man to never desire such an experience. The one that is guided by the Lord, on the other hand, experiences so much plenty that the bones are fat and strong.

The picture of a watered garden is a very refreshing one for the child of God. The one that is led of God is brought into a situation where he is full of life. A watered garden never lacks the basic ingredient for lusciousness: water. Whatever is sown in that garden surely comes out good. Flowers in a watered garden are beautiful and full of great scent; fruits in a watered garden are well formed and succulent. As long as the waters do not fail, these wonderful characteristics of things in the garden do not cease.

In your life, God wants you to be like a watered garden, where you will not only have the best of nourishment for your spirit, soul, and body, and be fruitful, but so you can be a blessing unto others also. Then let Him be your guide on an ongoing basis.

You Have a Heavenly Guide

For this God is our God for ever and ever: he will
be our guide even unto death.
—Psalm 48:14, kjv

From the beginning of God's relationship with His
people He has always made them to know that He is
willing to guide them. The patriarch Abraham was
told by God to leave his father's land, his people, and
his father's house for a land God would show him. The
very point of God in the matter is that Abraham would
learn and understand that the walk with God is absolutely dependent on His guidance. The children of Israel
also, by the time they left Egypt and were on the way to
the Promised Land, were guided by the pillar of cloud by
day and the pillar of fire by night.

You are not alone. You have a heavenly Guide
to revert to. It is all a matter of trust. Tell me what
prompted the wise men from the East first to isolate a
star that was on the move, much unlike all other stars
they had seen before, and also to follow the star. Call it
curiosity. If you have ever wondered what is in store for
your precious life, what ultimate end you were meant
to fulfill on Earth, then you should be willing to go to
God as your guide.

Much more, you must be willing to call on this Guide
to lead you. You do not need to do it on your own; you
can call on Him. Then you can be sure the journey will
end at the appointed destination. Besides, you can be
sure that you will not fall into the snares and traps on
the way; you will not have to go through the journey
with much harm to your soul.

God's Holy Spirit is the Guide of the child of God. The joy of the dispensation of those saved by the blood of Jesus is that the Spirit now dwells within us. So, help is not as far away as it used to be once He is called forth from heaven to help. By His quiet inner witness He can show us the way out of every cul-de-sac and bring us unto a good land.

BE LED BY THE SPIRIT

And Moses said to the Lord, If Your Presence does not go with me, do not carry us up from here!
—EXODUS 33:15, AMP

Moving without God is asking for trouble. Who can tell better than Moses? The first move he made in acknowledging that he was to lead the children of Egypt into deliverance was killing an Egyptian who assaulted a child of Israel. This act made him a fugitive for forty years. He spent a third of his entire lifetime at the backside of the desert because he would not ask God to lead him in what to do. It is even more precarious when the task to be done is ordained by God Himself. How would one carry out an assignment specifically ordered by the Lord without asking Him how it should be done?

Moving with God is a source of blessing. Having learned his lesson, Moses was ready now to ask God what He desired. Then God told him to go and meet his brother Aaron and both of them would appear before Pharaoh, and there, Moses would throw down his rod... Specific details were given to him, and the venture was a huge success to the very end of their leaving Egypt. When they had left Egypt and were well on the way to the Promised Land, Moses gave the assurance to God that they would not leave that place until they were sure of God's presence to guide them (Exod. 33:15).

Knowing that God is with us is our greatest asset. His Spirit is His Presence. He will guide us by His Spirit. Your declaration should always be, "I want what God wants for me. I desire the plan of God for my life!" If this is true, then you cannot help but seek Him for His guidance.

Don't move until you are sure that God has spoken. Then you can expect His blessing.

GOD PROMISES TO INSTRUCT YOU

> I [the Lord] will instruct you and teach you in the way you should go; I will counsel you with My eye upon you.
> —PSALM 32:8, AMP

Instructions are tools of guidance; they are the building blocks of life. That is why the Bible says in Proverbs 12:1 that the one who hates instruction is not better than an animal, because he is incapable of being guided; even animals are learning to follow instructions when they have been tamed.

God wants to guide you along the best pathway for your life, hence He gives you instructions. The entire Bible is a book of instructions; some have followed these instructions and the successes in their lives are on record both within the book and in contemporary history; some others have refused to follow the instructions and their woes too are in the book as well as in contemporary history. There is a choice for you as to what you would do with His instructions.

The Lord your God wants to direct you in the way you should go. God said to Joshua when he was to lead the people of Israel into the Promised Land that he had not gone that way before and should wait for His instructions. Each day is like a new wilderness for a child of God to go through unto his land of promise. Give God your hand and let Him lead you.

God promises: "I *will* instruct you!" So, go before Him early and receive instructions for your day. He is willing; you must be willing too. His counsels are His commandments, and though He does not enforce them upon any individual, the wise person takes them as laws that must be followed. Love God's instructions and desire them for your own good.

DIVINE DIRECTION

> Thus says the LORD, your Redeemer, The Holy One of Israel: "I am the LORD your God, Who teaches you to profit, Who leads you by the way you should go."
>
> —ISAIAH 48:17

King Cyrus was a heathen king whom God chose to use as a special vessel in the deliverance of His people. He knew nothing about the God of Israel and so God began to reveal Himself to him. It is very interesting, therefore, that at the very early stage of that relationship God was already telling Cyrus of His willingness to teach him His ways and to lead Cyrus in the way he should go.

His ways always lead to profit. It can be reasoned out that if God leads one in a particular way, then God is held bound to ensure that the way is successful and prosperous. In fact, He had to assure Cyrus that He would weaken other kings and their nations, "loosening their loins," so that Cyrus would be successful. Furthermore, Cyrus was assured that the king and nation that would not serve him would be destroyed.

Remember, He is your God. He will teach you what the best thing is for you. If you want to embark on a course of action or there is a project to be done, let Him teach you the profitable way. Especially as the Word of God says in Proverbs 14:12 and echoed in Proverbs 16:25 that there is a way that seems right unto a man in his eyes but the end of such a way is death, it behooves the child of God to learn to go to God for the profitable way, the way of life.

He will direct you and show you which way to go. He loves you and He cares for you. He is your Redeemer and He is interested in bringing you away from danger and harm and in settling you in a good land. Seek His divine direction.

In Exodus 13:21, the Bible says, "And the LORD went before them by day in a pillar of cloud to lead the way, and by night in a pillar of fire to give them light, so as to go by day and night." Just as God led the people in the Bible, He will lead you. Day and night, God led His people. No matter what season you are in, He wants to lead you. As you consider the future, remember your God will guide you.

HE WILL LEAD YOU

They shall come with weeping, And with supplications I will lead them. I will cause them to walk by the rivers of waters, In a straight way in which

they shall not stumble; For I am a Father to Israel,
And Ephraim is My firstborn.

—JEREMIAH 31:9

Sometimes man does not recognize that there is a God who is willing to guide him until he has reached his wits' end. Yet the love of God is so deep for us that He is willing to restore joy unto us in such circumstances.

Many situations bring man unto sorrow and tears. We cause a lot of pain unto ourselves when we choose to go our own way rather than ask God for the right way. *Bethlehem* means in the Hebrew language "the house of bread." Then there was famine in the supposed house of bread because of the evil of the people. God withdrew bread so they could come to an understanding of their wickedness and turn away from it. But as it is recorded in the Book of Ruth, Elimelech, who was of the lineage of the Levites—who were meant to understand God's ways—chose to abandon Bethlehem and went to Moab with his wife and two sons. If there would have been any change in the situation of the land, the Levites and priests would have been in the front line of that call for change, but Moab felt it better to abandon the land altogether. In Moab, he died and his two sons died. The only survivor, Naomi, eventually returned to Bethlehem, which was now full of bread by the time of her return.

So much sorrow and tears followed that move. In human terms, it is good thinking for a man to take his family to where there is bread, but that man did not know death was waiting in the very place where abundant provisions were. Those who waited in the house of bread and repented of their evil ways eventually received the mercy of God, and bread began to flow again. In fact, it was at a harvest season that Naomi returned. When the people called her name, she replied that there was no more beauty in the name as the name Naomi implies but that her life was full of bitterness. She returned in sorrow, but the story would take a turn for the better as she sought her God again with Ruth, who had earlier testified of that God as being worthy of worship. Naomi would go down in history as a woman in the lineage of the Messiah, Jesus, for she was the grandmother of Obed, who was the father of Jesse, who was the father of David the king.

God always has good things in store for each one of us. We all face challenges in the course of life. But God wants to bring us through these things to a better place. He will lead you home and He will care for you.

GOD IS YOUR SHEPHERD

But He made His own people go forth like sheep,
And guided them in the wilderness like a flock.
—PSALM 78:52

God is your shepherd and He wants to lead you. Though you may be like sheep, humble and innocent of the dangers of this world, lacking strength and worldly wisdom to handle affairs of this life, God as your shepherd would make you to progress and be successful still. By His guidance He will take you to a glorious end.

There was a time long ago that autistic children were declared unfit for learning and simply taken away from school. But thank God, today we have learned that with careful guidance these wonderful children can excel too, like their peers. God is gentle with us in all of our weaknesses, and that is why when He leads us, He knows our frame—that we are dust—and He carefully brings us to a desired end. It was David who testified in Psalm 18:35 that God's gentleness had made him great. When he remembered that he was not reckoned with among his father's children as anyone who could amount to a thing, he was quick to give the credit of his greatness to God, his shepherd.

So, David sang in Psalm 23 that the Lord was his shepherd, hence he lacked nothing. God wants to be your gentle shepherd and your closest friend. Though the whole world should consider you as nothing, God is ready to gently lead you in your life. He is the One who ordained your life and He can take you through the somewhat feeble steps till you get to your land of greatness.

Life can be difficult with its challenges and issues. But God wants to guide you safely through the hurdles of life. Life may appear like a maze with its confounding paths, but with God, everything is as clear as day. All you need to do is put your hand in His hands and enjoy a great walk.

Jesus said in John 10:11, "I am the good shepherd. The good shepherd gives His life for the sheep." The elements of faithfulness and truth should always fascinate you there. In the first instance, He is good. So you can trust that wherever He takes you can never be to your harm. Because He is good, He is seeking your own good in His guidance. Even when He had to give up His own life for your good, He did not restrain Himself from doing so. You can thrust your life on such a shepherd absolutely!

The wilderness is full of all kinds of dangers: serpents

and lions, bears and bandits. Many shepherds would flee at the very sight of danger and leave the sheep helpless to the invader; some shepherds tend the flock only to cruelly kill them for their own pleasures—but not your Shepherd. He will do all that is necessary to guarantee your life and well-being. He even laid down His life for you and for me. He will care for you always.

HE WILL LEAD, GUIDE, AND INSTRUCT YOU

> I will instruct you and teach you in the way you should go; I will guide you with My eye.
> —PSALM 32:8

The eyes of God see far and wide. The eyes of God do not only see the physical things perceived by men, but also the invisible things. The eyes of God see the intents and desires of the hearts of men, which are not perceivable by ordinary eyes.

When a man contemplates and plots things in his heart against someone, only God is able to deliver that person from the evil intended; hence, God says He will guide us with His eyes. How comforting! We can rely on what God has seen; there is no other information needed in the situation that is not immediately available to God.

God is with you every step of the way. He does not change like a shifting shadow. He will never leave you nor will He forsake you. He will lead, guide, and instruct you in each step you take.

You need to pray like the psalmist in Psalm 25:4, "Show me Your ways, O LORD; Teach me Your paths." We all need God's guidance in our lives. The lyrics of an old hymn say, "Guide me, O Thou great Jehovah."[2] In His greatness, the almighty God will guide us. It is great joy to be able to ask Him to do that because we are His people.

BE SENSITIVE TO HIS LEADING

Hear [O Jerusalem] the word of the Lord, you rulers or judges of [another] Sodom! Give ear to the law and the teaching of our God, you people of [another] Gomorrah!

—ISAIAH 1:10, AMP

It is vital that we pay attention to what God is saying to us. In an age where attention is being lost to instant machines and fast video games, the believer must develop ways to pay attention to what God is saying. God's instructions often come with specific details of which an individual must take note. Ask Moses and he would tell you he wished he had been more attentive to the words of God's instructions at the incident of the beating of the rock. God's words instructed Moses to point his rod at the rock and the rock would bring forth water. Because of the anger he was experiencing, Moses did not pay attention to those words and assumed that he was to smite the rock as he had done before. He missed getting to the Promised Land.

God often uses our situations and circumstances to speak to us. Many have said that God does not speak to them. They were expecting to hear the audible voice. The Holy Spirit dwells in the believer today, and much of the speaking is an inner witness in our heart or mind.

---

2   William Williams, "Guide me, O Thou great Jehovah," 1745. Public domain.

We might come into a situation or circumstance, and as we ponder on it, we receive an inspiration as to its meaning and purpose. God is speaking.

We need to be sensitive to His leading in our lives. Just as those in the medical profession learn to listen to the heartbeat, so should a believer learn to listen to God. How do you know God has spoken? During your personal study time you might have encountered a word in the Scriptures which has given you great enlightenment as to how God relates to His people, and in the course of the day, you experience a thing and your mind flashes to the word you encountered earlier. Has God spoken to you? Many dangers have passed over the children of God in circumstances as this; many insights into the appropriate action to be taken had come to children of God in similar situations. Respond to God and obey what He tells you to do.

WALK IN THE LIGHT OF HIS KINGDOM

Giving thanks to the Father who has qualified us to be partakers of the inheritance of the saints in the light. He has delivered us from the power of darkness and conveyed us into the kingdom of the Son of His love.

—COLOSSIANS 1:12–13

People stumble in darkness because visibility is poor. The enemy loves darkness because it hides traps and pits, and it is easy to ensnare people in the dark. God's answer to the enemy's evil schemes is to shine His light for His people to walk. Walk in the light of God!

You have been rescued by God Himself. Once you were part of those who sit in darkness and in the shadow of death. Isaiah 9:2 says that the people who walked in darkness have seen a great light and they that dwell in the land of the shadow of death, upon them has the light shined. God has rescued you from the power of darkness.

Don't allow darkness and wickedness to overcome you or influence you again. Walk in the light of His Kingdom. One thing about darkness is that it is simply the absence of light. Darkness does not need any invitation; it comes in naturally when the light is switched off. The Lord guides us by His light, and darkness cannot understand the light of God. This is your key to prevailing over evil.

It is the will of God that you will not stumble in darkness nor grope like the blind in darkness. He will guide you.

GUIDED BY DESTINY

> You saw me before I was born and scheduled each day of my life before I began to breathe. Every day was recorded in your book!
> —PSALM 139:16, TLB

People often refer to the journey of life as a maze, and that is true. It is also true that the Constructor of the maze knows everything about it and can guide one successfully through it. God is this Constructor and He will guide you to your destination.

David had an insight into the plans God already ordained before time began for every individual's life on Earth. Isn't it wonderful to know that God is thinking about us! David talked about the scheduling of his days. Just as an individual makes a to-do list or a timetable,

God has made a schedule of your life. It is only wise to let Him guide you through life.

Each day is a day planned by God for you. David said each day is recorded in God's book. How will this record read at the end of today or at the end of your life? You should take advantage of each day. Little wonder David said in Psalm 118:24, "This is the day which the LORD hath made; we will rejoice and be glad in it" (KJV). Take advantage of today! Let your joy and gladness come forth in this day.

LORD, I PLACE MY HAND IN YOUR HAND TODAY

For I, the LORD your God, will hold your right hand, Saying to you, "Fear not, I will help you."
—ISAIAH 41:13

Every man at his best still needs help in one area or the other. The help that is available unto a man is as effective and valuable as the person offering the help. For example, if a man is confronted by those who want to beat him up and one weak old lady says she is going to help, it is clear that both the helper and the person being helped would suffer injuries.

When God offers His help, however, you can rejoice that everything shall be all right for you. Whatever has been the cause of fear and anxiety disappears before the awesomeness of God. But He extends His hands to you for the help to begin. Are you ready to put your hands in His hands?

God wants to lead us every step of the way. However, you must trust Him to do so and give Him your hand to hold. Then the guidance and help can begin. Imagine

God taking hold of your hand! This is a great way to live. If God is holding us up, we will not fall.

WAIT ON THE LORD

> I waited patiently for the LORD. He turned to me and heard my cry for help.
>
> —PSALM 40:1, GW

> The steps of a good man are ordered by the LORD, And He delights in his way.
>
> —PSALM 37:23

However desperate a situation may look, it is advisable not to take a step without God's guidance, especially because the enemy uses the distraction of urgency and desperation to lure one into his traps.

It takes all patience to wait on the Lord. It is not because the affairs of this world and other elements in the galaxies have kept God so busy that He cannot attend to you; it is because He knows the appropriate time that the blessing would do the utmost in your life. So wait on the Lord.

God wants to direct your life. God wants to show you which way to go. God is interested in every step you take. Don't take a step without Him.

The fact that we can call on God is a wonderful privilege. It is even more gratifying to know that He is delighted at every move we make. And because He delights in our ways, He wants to order our steps aright. That is why we need to wait patiently for Him to do the ordering for effective results. A child of God should not be rash in making decisions or taking actions; the guidance of God would determine the proper decision or action in various circumstances. God is a faithful Father and He will guide unto victory, glory, and greatness.

Praying Points

Prayer: *Lord, I pray that You will guide me. I pray that You will satisfy me, even when my circumstances seem to be a challenge. In Jesus's name, amen.*

Prayer: *Lord, help me to be patient as I continue to call on You and trust in You for an outcome to my situation. In Jesus's name, amen.*

Prayer: *Lord, I ask for Your leading and guidance in my life. Lead, guide, and direct me I pray and show me which way to go. In Jesus's name, amen.*

Declaration: *I want what God wants for me. I desire the plan of God for my life!*

Prayer: *Lord, You are God and my life is in Your hands. Fulfill Your purposes in my life and bring Your plans for my life to pass. In Jesus's name, amen.*

Prayer: *Lord, I desire that You would lead me and show me what I need to do. You know best and You have plans for my life. Help me not to settle for anything less. In Jesus's name, amen.*

Prayer: *Lord, I ask You to lead and guide me in the decisions I need to make. Make it clear to me what I need to do in each situation, I pray. In Jesus's name, amen.*

Prayer: *Lord, teach me what I need to know and show me the way in which I should go. In Jesus's name, amen.*

Prayer: *Lord, I know that You can use and give purpose to all the issues I face. Thank You that You are my Father and You will help me. In Jesus's name, amen.*

Prayer: *Lord, be my guide and my shepherd through every circumstance that I may face. Fill me with Your peace and preserve my life, I pray. In Jesus's name, amen.*

Prayer: *Lord, You are my God and You are my Good Shepherd. You care for me and I know this is true! In Jesus's name, amen.*

Prayer: *Lord, I realize that I cannot do it on my own. I need You. I place my life and future in Your hands, and I ask You to show me which way to go in every aspect of my life. In Jesus's name, amen.*

Prayer: *Lord, I pray that You will lead me and guide me and show me which way I need to go. In Jesus's name, amen.*

Prayer: *Lord, it is my desire to follow and do what You want me to do. Help me to learn as You teach me and help me to follow You. In Jesus's name, amen.*

Prayer: *Lord, thank You for the wonderful work You have done in my life. My life is changed because of what You have done for me. In Jesus's name, amen.*

Prayer: *Lord, You are so faithful! You bring me through the tough seasons and help me so that I will not stumble or fall. In Jesus's name, amen.*

Prayer: *Lord, I celebrate the fact that You made me and You have a plan and a purpose for my life. In Jesus's name, amen.*

Prayer: *Lord, I place my hand in Your hand today. I pray that You will lead me and guide me in all my choices and attitudes. In Jesus's name, amen.*

Prayer: *Lord, I ask that You would lead and guide me in every step I need to take today and in this New Year. Show me which way to go, I pray. In Jesus's name, amen.*

Chapter 9

ALL NEEDS MET BY HIS STRENGTH

He Is All We Need

*Whom have I in heaven but thee? and there is
none upon earth that I desire beside thee.*

—PSALM 73:25, KJV

AVE YOU HAVE heard people say that you need to
have someone in the right places to connect you
into things? David had someone, and in the right
places too. The two major spheres of life are heaven
and earth, and the person that is reckoned with in both
places is the man! No wonder David reigned as king on
Earth, and in heaven, the King of kings was reckoned
with David's lineage as well.

God is our absolute necessity. It is easy to recognize
systems that are evil and demonic. Anytime you find a
system that wants to make God irrelevant in the lives
of men, you don't need to look further for the operations of the devil. Lucifer contended for the throne in
heaven, and since he was cast down, his activities are
very much in contention with the sovereignty and glory
of God. You need God and you need to make Him see
that He is wanted in your life.

BE STRENGTHENED WITH ALL MIGHT

When you know God as a living reality then you will discover that you need Him. The lie of the devil is to make man see God as a force or an influence; God is a Person and you need to relate to Him as such. When you are able to see Him in everyday life, then you will learn to reckon with Him in all of your affairs.

Sooner or later we realize that we have no one else to turn to but God. No doubt there are good men on Earth, but situations occur that good men would want to help but they cannot. Good men can provide all the funding for the treatment of cancer or heart-related problems but they cannot make the cancer go away or stop the heart from collapsing. At such a time we discover that He is all we need.

He is all you need. When you have made all preparations and have built yourself up in education and all other ways, you still come across situations that are simply beyond your ability to handle. Paul's testimony of this God makes it clear in 2 Corinthians 12:9: "Each time he said, 'No. But I am with you; that is all you need. My power shows up best in weak people.' Now I am glad to boast about how weak I am; I am glad to be a living demonstration of Christ's power, instead of showing off my own power and abilities" (TLB).

Whatever you are facing today, He is all you need! Whatever you may go through tomorrow, He is all you need! Whatever you have been battling with for a long time, He is all you need! Whatever you are contending with right now, He is all you need! He is *all* you need.

HE PROMISED TO MEET YOUR NEEDS

The young lions lack and suffer hunger; but those
who seek the LORD shall not lack any good thing.
—PSALM 34:10

The mastery and dominion of the king of the jungle is
not in contention. If anyone contends it, such may not
live to write the story. However, age sets in; the lion gets
old and weak, unable to pursue game and establish its
dominion like before. Strength fails the old lion, but
not the young ones! They are quick to the spring, agile
and able to move their bodies swiftly as they pursue
and pounce on their game. But what happens when the
game is not accessible?

David understood this and he sang the praise of God
in Psalm 104:27–29 for how provisions are made for all
of God's creations when God opens His hands, but when
He turns His back, all are troubled. So the competent
and prepared, the connected and socially mobile, and all
those who are comfortable of their abilities and qualities
can only operate as far as they are given the opportunities by God. God is all everyone needs.

When we understand that He is all we need, then we
seek Him. To seek means to inquire, call, request, ask,
and pray to. If you have a need, you have the right to call
on God. Everyone does have a need, whether it is emotional, psychological, financial, political, social, or whatever form of need. Based on the authority of God's Word,
when you call on God, expect His answer. The promise
is that those who seek the Lord will lack no good thing.

Good things come in various shapes and sizes to different individuals. While a child may desire a burger as a good thing, a father might desire a car. While college education is a good thing to one teenager, another may desire placement on the soccer team. A political office may be a good thing to a man while to another the good thing is being able to house the homeless people on the streets. Whatever that good thing is, the promise of God is that you will not lack it. So step forward and get it from Him. Seek Him today.

Praying Points

Prayer: *Lord, today I give You the final control in my life. I declare that You are my desire and the longing of my heart. In Jesus's name, amen.*

Prayer: *Thank You, Lord, that You are all I need. I will place my confidence and trust in You for this new week. In Jesus's name, amen.*

Prayer: *Lord, it is reassuring to know that You hear me when I call and You promise to meet my needs. In Jesus's name, amen.*

Chapter 10

THE END OF STRENGTH IS PEACE

Life Is a Race and a Fight

For who is God, except the LORD? And who is a rock, except our God? It is God who arms me with strength, and makes my way perfect.

—PSALM 18:31—32

L IFE IS A race and a fight. But the understanding of this has been twisted in the hearts of men and has led to ugly rivalry and unhealthy competitions. So we face all kinds of challenges arising from this wrong perception and corresponding attitude. Nonetheless, the reality is that these challenges come upon us in our daily walk.

Life is a race. It is a race that is meant to be run by every individual on his own course and on his own terms. The way another person runs his race is only meant to be an encouragement, an insight and a boost toward your running your own race. But man has turned the race against one another, and so they pull down the other, put obstacles on the path of the other, and even desire that the other be removed totally from the face of the earth.

Life is a fight, a fight against the elements on Earth that hinder the fulfillment of one's purpose. When God made man, He blessed him with the power to subdue the earth and to be in dominion. The fight a man should fight is to overcome the challenges in nature that would not make a man accomplish his goals and fulfill his destiny. But men have taken the fight to one another. They are more interested in subduing men and enslaving others than in subduing the earth.

Each day we have to stand and embrace the challenges imposed upon us by such attitudes of men in our world. But we are not alone. God is with us. Our peace is the ultimate end of the strength He provides for us in the battles of life. God will fight for you, and you shall hold your peace.

Peace Be With You

Now as they said these things, Jesus Himself stood in the midst of them, and said to them, "Peace to you."

—LUKE 24:36

The apostles were in distress; their Master had been crucified, helpless and shameless like a criminal. They were in confusion; what would their lives amount to now that the Master who shook the nation and gave them recognition and honor was gone from them? Greater bewilderment overtook them when they began to hear of the Master being alive. In this state of utter despair, Jesus appeared physically in their midst and said, "Peace to you."

This is how the peace of God is given to every child

of His. There is enough going on in the world today to shake us: disasters and rumors of war, terrorist attacks and train wrecks. To drive it closer to home, you cannot guarantee a safe return of your child from school without news of gunshots or a bus hijack or molestation by one lewd fellow. Yet it is not the will of God for you to live your life in fear and anxiety. He gives you peace because He is there to watch over everyone and everything that concerns you.

Life also has its fair share of storms: the issues that confront the family and want to tear down the sacred institution, financial issues that leave you distraught, health matters that try your best wits and strength. But in all these things, God gives us His peace.

The apostles looked into the face of Jesus and peace flooded their hearts. They were convinced that whatever power made their Master rise from the dead in spite of all the horrible passion He had witnessed, that power was able to sustain them in life. Look into the face of your Savior and receive His peace. He has made that power, the Holy Ghost, available for you too. You shall not be comfortless.

My Hiding Place

You are my hiding place; You shall preserve me from trouble; You shall surround me with songs of deliverance.

—Psalm 32:7

Children love hide-and-seek. A father and his son especially loved to play the game. But war came one day and armed people stormed their house and wiped out everyone within sight, adults and children alike. They searched everywhere to be sure that they had cleaned up after them, but they missed the little boy because he was in a hiding place.

One night in the land of Egypt, the angel of death came visiting. The angel had received his orders: all first-borns of men and beast were to be wiped out of the land. But the children of Israel were dwelling in the same land at Goshen. The angel could not get to them because they were in a hiding place. The blood of the Passover lamb that they had smeared on their homes shielded them from the destruction by the angel of death.

You have a sacred hideaway too, Someone under whom you can hide in times of trouble. David under-stands this message literally and otherwise. When King Saul chased him from hole to cave, except the Lord had been his hiding place in the wide dragnet that Saul spread, his life would have been snuffed out. When his spiritual enemy came for his life, too, in the issue of the death of Uriah and the adultery with Bathsheba, death could have been the fierce judgment upon him; but the mercy of God hid him away and took only the product of the adultery.

God even wants to preserve you from trouble. It would be naive for someone to think that troubles cannot come to him. Job declared in Job 14:1 that man who is born of a woman is of few days and full of trouble! It is much more a matter of *when* than a matter of *if.* When it hap-pens, where will you hide? David was sure of his own hiding place, and he confidently declared in Psalm 91:1, "He who dwells in the secret place of the Most High shall abide under the shadow of the Almighty." Storms will come but God will be there for you.

Paul admonished the brethren in Colossians 3:15, "And let the peace of God rule in your hearts, to which also you were called in one body; and be thankful." God has called us to peace. It is a holy calling and we are to come under this hiding place with gratitude to God that we are safe from the evils of this world.

God Is With You

> Yea, though I walk through the valley of the shadow of death, I will fear no evil; For You are with me; Your rod and Your staff, they comfort me.
> —PSALM 23:4

David was a warrior. That was his calling before God, to showcase the glory of God in the victories he had. His fight against Goliath and the Philistines all lend credence to his calling as a warrior. Even God acknowledged it and told him that his hands were full of blood, thus he could not build the house of God as his heart desired. But to think you are not a warrior like David is to show ignorance of the spiritual world around you. Everyone is engaged in a war; the forces of darkness bring the battle to your home and endeavors and they don't negotiate with you in the matter.

But your sure haven is that God is with you, and you are more than a conqueror and an overcomer. If God is with you then you do not need to fear. Some situations in life are a hair's breadth of death: accidents on the road that happen suddenly and without notice, a sudden collapse of a building when you are passing by... Jesus was told in Luke 13:1 of some Galileans who went to offer sacrifice and were slain by Pilate, who mixed their blood with the blood of their sacrifice. He cautioned the people not to think those ones were the worst sinners on Earth.

Self-righteousness might rob you of the cover of God. It is the presence of God rather than your good works that qualifies you for safe keeping in God's hiding place. There is a greater closeness with God that we can enjoy when we seek unto Him. God wants to protect and guide us

FILL ME WITH YOUR PEACE

> For God is not the author of confusion but of peace, as in all the churches of the saints.
> —1 Corinthians 14:33

The owner, the original title holder to a work is the author. You may also see the author as the source, the fount from which the whole thing flows. God is not the author of confusion. He has no part in that which confounds or brings confusion. The Bible says in James 3:16 that where envying and strife is, there is confusion and every evil work. From this you can deduce who the author of confusion is: the devil.

But God is the Author of peace. There is a popular bumper sticker that reads, "Know Christ, know peace; no Christ, no peace." He is the Owner, the Fountain from which peace flows. He said unto His people in John 14:27, "My peace I give to you; not as the world gives." How does the world give its peace? The world gives relief from threats and attacks as long as you comply with their orders, but Jesus gives peace like a river. Jesus gives peace which overflows and which is not dependent on the good behavior of the receiver.

So don't allow yourself to be agitated or disturbed. Do not permit yourselves to be fearful, intimidated, or unsettled. Reach forward and take hold of His gift of peace.

He is the God of peace. Where He is allowed to be God, peace will reign. So let Him be God in your marriage, let Him be God in your business, let Him be God in your group, and let Him be God in your community; let Him be God in all areas of your life. Whatever area of your life you shield away from Jesus, you are inviting the author of confusion into that portion of your life. The terrible thing with the devil is that he is not satisfied with taking hold of that portion which you yield to him; he wants all of you. That is why the Scriptures admonish us not to give room to the devil; you give him an inch, and he does not want just a mile—he wants everything.

Today, Jesus extends His peace to you. It is a free gift; receive it now!

Speak Your Peace into My Situation

> But He said to them, "Why are you fearful, O you of little faith?" Then He arose and rebuked the winds and the sea, and there was a great calm.
> —Matthew 8:26

Tossed by tempest, inconsolable and fearful, the disciples cried out to Jesus one day, "Do you not care that we are perishing?" (Mark 4:38). The Prince of Peace was sleeping in a part of the boat in which all of them were travelling. Whether the "we" under reference here included Jesus, we might not find out until we get to heaven; but if it did and He was the One who ordered the trip that brought them unto that situation, the guys might as well have been saying Jesus brought them all on a suicide bid! If it doesn't, it makes matters even worse; He could have well been labeled a murderer.

But Jesus was going to take His disciples through another of the lessons He wanted them to know. As they say, experience is the best teacher. If Jesus had told them that a mortal could manifest in the power that controls the elements of this world, this bunch of fishermen would probably sneer and ask Him to tell them other fables. But at His word, wind and sea obeyed Him that day. That must have been something none of them could ever forget, especially Philip on the day he found himself caught up by the wind into the wilderness and suddenly found himself with the Ethiopian eunuch (see Acts 8:26–40).

When God speaks, things happen. God spoke and the winds and the waves were still. Job gave a secret about troubles that every believer needs to know. Job said in Job 5:6–8 (KJV), "Although affliction cometh not forth of the dust, neither doth trouble spring out of the ground; Yet man is born unto trouble, as the sparks fly upward. I would seek unto God, and unto God would I commit my cause." Job was saying that troubles just seem to appear from nowhere, and before one knows it, all tranquility is gone and one is battling for life. But in the words of Job, one can find a sweet relief: troubles are like sparks of fire flying upward. They make one fear as one hears the cackling of the sparks in fire and the red flames going upward; but what happens minutes after? They fizzle out!

But oftentimes with our fear and anxiety we provide new stubble for the sparks to land on and continue the fire. Fear not! The Prince of Peace is in the boat of your life and no evil can happen to you. He is powerful and can calm the storms in your life. Let Him restore peace and calm to your troubled heart.

STRENGTH AND PEACE

The LORD will give strength to His people; the LORD will bless His people with peace.
—PSALM 29:11

Here are two great treasures that God has for you: strength and peace. God gives strength that peace may ensue in your life. A classical example of this is the story of Elisha and the Syrian troops in 2 Kings 6:13–23. The king of Syria had been strategizing how to overrun the army of Israel, but every strategy he had was revealed by God unto Elisha, and Elisha would warn the king of Israel and the strategy would fail. In frustration, the king of Syria accused his lieutenants that someone had been leaking his secrets to the people of Israel. They told the king that it was not quite so, but that Elisha heard even the things that the king discussed in his bedchamber! So the king of Syria sent a great army to arrest Elisha.

But supernatural strength was given to Elisha, and he commanded the entire army to be blind and they all went blind. Elisha then took them to the king of Israel, whom he told not to harm them but to feed them and send them back to their master. It is no surprise, therefore, that after this incident the Bible records that the army of Syria never came to Israel again. The peace the people of Israel enjoyed came with the strength God gave to Elisha. As for you too, the Lord shall give you strength to prevail over your enemies and they will never trouble you again.

Be Patient in Trouble

Be glad for all God is planning for you. Be patient in trouble, and prayerful always.
—Romans 12:12, tlb

Every article on the shelf has an expiration date. Trouble is a commodity put in the marketplace by the devil, and as he himself has an expiration date, so does his commodity. That is why the Bible admonishes us to be patient, for the trouble will soon be taken down and destroyed from the shelves. As long as you don't buy it and own it, the devil's commodity shall surely be taken out of your life.

What makes it easier for a child of God to exercise patience? It is the thought and indeed the assurance that God is planning something that is not altogether plain to you at the moment, but which will soon show fully. That is why with gladness you can wait for the Lord's plans for your life to fully materialize.

So what should you be doing while waiting? Pray! Praise the Lord who has such a great plan for your life. Ask Him to frustrate the evil works of the enemy and to fulfill the plan absolutely. God has so much planned out for each of us. This should give us hope and expectation.

We will face troubles, but ultimately God has good

things in store. We need to go to God in prayer and ask that He releases the good things in His store. Do not patronize the devil's commodity, but patiently receive the deliverance of God and be at peace.

LET YOUR SOUL BE AT PEACE

> Therefore do not worry and be anxious...your heavenly Father knows well that you need them all [from day to day].
> —MATTHEW 6:31–32, AMP

Sometimes you want to say to God, "Are You kidding me?" The moments that God tells you not to worry are the very moments your adrenaline wants to fly out through your ears! The children of Israel were fenced off from advancing forward by the Red Sea and the fiercest army on earth was advancing on them with every intention of vengeance, and guess what God says? "Fear not"!

Well, don't blame God; He is not toying with your life nor is He interested in making your emotions go sour. It's simply because He has access to some information of which you are not aware. How easy is it to try and explain to a child that all the liquid stuff being mixed in a bowl will soon harden up and become a delicious cake? All the child wants is the end product. And there are times when explanations would not even hold water in the ears of the fearful! So God simply calms everybody down, or shall we say, tries to calm everybody down, with a "Fear not."

God is your heavenly Father. He knows your needs and He knows how to supply your needs. Beyond your understanding of the situation, God does not only have a perfect understanding of it, He already knew how it would all end, even before you came into the world. So give Him your fears and anxieties. Let your soul be at peace, the Lord is on your side.

MAY THE LORD GIVE YOU PEACE

The LORD lift up his countenance upon thee, and give thee peace.

—NUMBERS 6:26, KJV

The Lord instructed Moses to pronounce the blessings that we call the apostolic blessing today upon the children of Israel. These are the blessings of provision, keeping, guidance, grace, favor, and finally peace. It is quite significant that the ultimate of these blessings is the blessing of peace; all the other blessings actually add up to the blessing of peace.

Peace as used in the Scriptures is more than just the absence of trouble; it is total well-being. The Lord wants to provide for you and keep you from all evil. He also wants to guide you in your journey of life and make His grace to be upon you so that what you don't merit still comes to you. Moreover, He wants to look upon you with favor; the Lord wants to show you His good face and favor you above all others. Let His light shine on you. Receive the gift of peace that He gives to you.

PRAYING POINTS

Prayer: *Lord, today, challenge and opportunity stand before us. We pray that today will be a day of destiny in our lives. Strengthen us we pray. In Jesus's name, amen.*

Prayer: *Lord, when I look to You, my heart is sure and confident. Help me not to take my eyes off You. In Jesus's name, amen.*

Prayer: *Lord, thank You that You are my hiding place from every storm that life may bring my way. You are my only security and I will trust You to keep and preserve my life. In Jesus's name, amen.*

Prayer: *Lord, in the storms and events of my life, I need Your peace. Help me to be guided with the peace that only comes from You. In Jesus's name, amen.*

Prayer: *Lord, thank You that You are leading and guiding me. I am so thankful that I have nothing to fear. In Jesus's name, amen.*

Prayer: *Lord, in the midst of a world that is troubled and afraid, I take this moment and I receive Your gift of peace in my life. Fill me with Your peace from the top of my head to the soles of my feet. In Jesus's name, amen.*

Prayer: *Lord, I come to You in the storms and hurdles of life. Speak Your peace into my situation, I pray. In Jesus's name, amen.*

Prayer: *Lord, I reach out right now and I receive the gifts of strength and peace that You have offered to me. I rejoice, knowing that You are able and You will enable me. In Jesus's name, amen.*

Prayer: *Lord, all my cares and concerns, I give to You right now. You are my Provider and I know You will provide for me. In Jesus's name, amen.*

Prayer: *Lord, thank You for Your peace which I now receive. Your peace is sure, even while storms may be raging around me. May Your peace silence my anxiety and distress now, I pray. In Jesus's name, amen.*

Prayer: *Lord, look upon me, Your child, with favor and blessing. Fill my heart and mind with the peace that comes from You alone. In Jesus's name, amen.*

Prayer: *Lord, when I look to You, my heart is sure and confident. Help me not to take my eyes off of You. In Jesus's name, amen.*

Chapter 11

COURAGE TO MOVE IN GOD'S STRENGTH

Be Encouraged

Finally, brethren, farewell (rejoice)! Be strengthened (perfected, completed, made what you ought to be); be encouraged and consoled and comforted; be of the same [agreeable] mind one with another; live in peace, and [then] the God of love [Who is the Source of affection, goodwill, love, and benevolence toward men] and the Author and Promoter of peace will be with you.

—2 Corinthians 13:11, AMP

OURAGE IS A virtue for success and fulfillment. It takes courage to make the needed move in the face of daunting oppositions. Even with the assurance of help from the most credible source and the guidance provided through the venture, a man would still need courage to make a success of the venture.

One instance when people need to be encouraged to do a thing is when such a thing has never been done before. The building of the ark in the wilderness had never been embarked upon on Earth, the building of Noah's ark had never been embarked upon on Earth, and the building of Solomon's temple had no blueprint on

Earth. You can then understand the amount of courage needed by the architects of these structures.

Even in circumstances where the project is not the first on Earth but what is needed to do is overwhelming it takes courage to take the first step. When Joshua already had the victory of crossing the River Jordan with the people of Israel, he was faced with the challenge of the wall of Jericho. This was a wall said to accommodate some chariots riding side by side on top of it: the width and the solidity of it were amazing and frightening. But as Joshua contemplated capturing Jericho, the Commander of the army of heaven appeared to him and courage returned.

God always wants to encourage you. As you face that seemingly insurmountable obstacle, God wants to build you up and strengthen you. You shall overcome it. He says: "Be strengthened, be encouraged and be comforted." Assured of His presence and His love, let us receive courage to face that challenge; we shall be victorious and our testimonies shall bring comfort to our lives and to others.

STRENGTHEN MY HEART

> Be of good courage, and He [the Lord] shall strengthen your heart.
>
> —PSALM 27:14

Courage is an element of faith; the one who musters courage believes that the strength of the Lord will not fail him. But it is interesting to note that the very strength that is needed in the matter is not given until the person has mustered the courage. Do you believe

God to do what you want to embark upon? Then show your courage and step forward. Strength will follow.

The children of Israel wanted to cross the Jordan River, and the instructions of God were that the water would part when the priests bearing the ark of the covenant had stepped into the river. Now, there is the problem. The priests have a choice to reason: What if the river does not part? So at what appears to be a risk to their lives, they stepped into the river. And the river parted; strength came when they had mustered the courage to step in.

Trust in the Lord. Have faith, do not despair. Be brave and courageous to make the move that God has ministered to your heart. What if nothing happens? But look at the converse of it: what if something happens! It was perhaps easier for the children of Israel at the Red Sea; the army of Pharaoh behind them was enough incentive to dare. But with Joshua, they simply had to make a choice to believe God or not to believe.

Believe in the Lord your God. Be of good courage and He will strengthen your heart.

BE STRONG AND OF GOOD COURAGE

> "Have I not commanded you? Be strong and of good
> courage; do not be afraid, nor be dismayed, for the
> LORD your God is with you wherever you go."
> —JOSHUA 1:9

Moses died and the mantle fell on Joshua. For the young man who had been close to Moses and knew that it was the stiff-necked people of Israel that sent Moses to his grave and his missing the Promised Land, Joshua needed something to carry out this mandate: strength and courage. It took God assuring Joshua three times at a meeting for Joshua to be willing to move. In fact, one could almost detect a tone of exasperation in the words of God here; such was the reluctance of Joshua to accept the mandate.

But the moment Joshua had an understanding that all he needed was the strength and courage not to fight the enemies of Israel or to lead the children of Israel, but to simply believe that God was with him, the rest was easy. The greatest strength and courage expected of a child of God is to believe God is with him in spite of what circumstances may show.

God is with us! The ultimate revelation of God is in His Son, Jesus Christ, and one should pay attention to the sum of this revelation in the name Emmanuel, meaning God with us. Believing God is with us makes us deal ruthlessly with fear and doubt. We must encourage ourselves to be bold and strong, because He is with us!

BE ENCOURAGED, YOU ARE ON THE WINNING SIDE

"Don't be afraid," the prophet answered. "Those who are with us are more than those who are with them."

—2 KINGS 6:16, NIV

Fear is a manifestation of a position of weakness; it is an acknowledgement that the contrary forces are able to overcome one. Such was the situation of Elisha and his servant when the king of Syria sent a whole army to arrest Elisha. Waking up early in the morning, the servant stepped out and saw a huge army waiting at the base of the mountain where he and his master Elisha were. He saw no means of escape and no way that such an army could be overcome; he cried in despair.

But his master Elisha saw the situation differently; he saw the army at the base of the mountain in peril of destruction! For there was another army, the heavenly host, which was on top of the mountain and around the entire perimeter. So he gave the assurance to the servant that those who were with them were more than those who were with the army below; more in number, more in strength and ability for warfare, more in all respects, for they were horses and chariots of fire, a heavenly host.

Life can give us many reasons to be fearful. Have you heard people say, "You do not know what I am going through"? Believe me, you do not know for real. Because even though you may know the circumstances and the details of the person's experience, you cannot see the situation through his eyes. Through his eyes, it is an impossible situation, it is a hopeless situation and it is insurmountable. Yet, let the individual know that we are not alone. Man may not be able to do a thing about it, but the One with us is awesome and terrible in battle.

God in His power and strength will reveal Himself. As the servant of Elisha received courage when he got a revelation of the army around them on top of the mountain, you will receive a revelation of your God that will strengthen your heart. Be encouraged, you are on the winning side.

Praying Points

Prayer: *Lord, I need Your encouragement and the strength that only You can give to be a reality in my life! In Jesus's name, amen.*

Prayer: *Lord, as I embrace this new day, help me to be strong and to take heart. Thank You that You will come alongside me and strengthen my heart. In Jesus's name, amen.*

Prayer: *Lord, I will be bold and strong in the strength that You give me. In Jesus's name, amen.*

Prayer: *Lord, help me not to be overcome with the things that appear to have the upper hand. Remind me that You are with me and that makes me a winner. In Jesus's name, amen.*

Chapter 12

STRENGTH THROUGH CONFIDENCE IN THE LORD

The Lord Is Your Confidence

For the Lord shall be your confidence, firm and strong, and shall keep your foot from being caught [in a trap or some hidden danger].

—PROVERBS 3:26, AMP

HAVE YOU SEEN a little kid taking his first few steps? While the child may be encouraged by the novelty of it all, he does not have an understanding about what the strength of his feet has to do with it all. He simply gains confidence after a few trials. Your confidence in the ability of God to take care of you is built up in the trials you take. If you have never believed God to hold you up anytime in your Christian journey, chances are you will never step out unto great things.

The Lord will keep and preserve you. There are traps and hidden dangers, yes; but to be paralyzed by the thought of these traps and hidden dangers is to miss what God has put in front of you. God is firm and strong, not careless, slothful, or shoddy as to miss doing what is necessary in your situation.

I see a clear distinction here between putting confidence in God and having God as your confidence. The former has to do with calling on God to help you as you do to men or institutions or whatever; but the latter implies that no one or nothing else other than God rules all affairs and ventures of your life. Let the Lord be your security and strength.

He wants to prevent you from falling into a trap. The trap has been set and the enemy merely waits for you to be caught in it; but God says He will keep your feet from being caught in that trap. He cares for you and so you can rely on Him.

He Is Workings Things Out for Your Good

For the Lord your God fights for you, just as he has promised. So...love the Lord your God.
—Joshua 23:10–11, NLT

Gideon asked the question in Judges 6:13 (KJV), "Oh my Lord, if the Lord be with us, why then is all this befallen us?" Many of us are at such crossroads today, asking where God is in the midst of our situations. He is working things out for your good.

At the same time, He is at work within us. The ultimate purpose of God is to accomplish a change in us. So while we wait to see things happen on the outside, God waits to see things happen on the inside. All the years David spent keeping the sheep in the wilderness, maybe he did not know that God was building him up to have value for life and for what was entrusted to his care. The day he chose to oppress Uriah by taking Uriah's wife simply because he could, he met with the fierce anger of God. Moses too was being built up in the wilderness to handle his anger, which was a result of his status and pride as son of Pharaoh's daughter, but the anger eventually denied him of the Promised Land.

Would the situation have been different with these two if they had allowed God to perfect His work in them? So while it may seem that God is not doing anything, have this understanding that He is at work in your life. Love Him for it, because the time that you will need the strength from what He is doing right now will come.

The Lord your God is fighting for you. He makes everything perfect in His time.

His Timing Is Always Perfect

> The Lord does not delay and is not tardy or slow about what He promises.
>
> —2 Peter 3:9, amp

Who has a better understanding of your destiny, you or God? The assessment of man as touching his position a particular issue depends on the pain, discomfort, or shame he is experiencing in the issue. His expectations concerning the issue also dictate to him whether the issue is being handled by God or not. These should not be our parameters for judging God.

The Lord is not slow to do what He has promised, as some think. He has a better understanding of things than we do. Which father either in love of his ten-year-old or in desire to be free from taking the child to school daily would give the key of his car to that child? God says in Galatians 4:1 that the heir, as long as he is a child, is not different in any manner from a servant, though he is lord of all the inheritance. God is therefore more interested in building you up first before releasing you into what He has promised.

He will do what He has promised He would do. Sometimes there is a delay and He may seem slow. But His timing is always perfect and He does not forget. Joseph would testify to the fact that God never forgets. Eighteen years after his dream, through danger of the pit to slavery and to prison, his dream eventually came to pass. God has not forgotten you.

Just hold on to God. It was a critical moment in the life of Jacob, the heir of the lineage of Abraham and Isaac. God had told him to return to his father's land after three decades in the house of Laban. He was returning to enter into his inheritance, but his brother Esau was a threat to his life.

Jacob sent all ahead of him and remained behind to seek unto God. The angel of God appeared to him, and after a struggle, Jacob declared in Genesis 32:26, 29, "'I will not let You go unless You bless me!'...And He blessed him [Jacob] there." While you are waiting for God to fulfill His promise, hold on to Him in prayers.

It is a good thing to desire God's blessing on our lives. But we should be relentless like Jacob. Jacob struggled with God and got God's blessing. He was determined to hold on to God. As we cling to God we can expect His blessing.

He will answer you. Isaiah 30:19 (KJV) says, "For the people shall dwell in Zion at Jerusalem: thou shalt weep no more: he will be very gracious unto thee at the voice of thy cry; when he shall hear it, he will answer thee." God is not going to disdain your cry unto Him;

He will not ignore your petitions before Him, for He is a good God!

He wants to be gracious and kind toward you. Call on Him; He hears. He will answer you.

I WILL BE CONFIDENT

> Though a host encamp against me, my heart shall not fear; though war arise against me, [even then] in this will I be confident.
> —PSALM 27:3, AMP

One commendable thing with David was that he knew where his confidence lay even before the challenges of his life came to him. He made his boast in the Lord his God as touching what He would do in his life irrespective of the situation. Verse 1 (AMP) of this passage finds David declaring, "The Lord is my light and my salvation—whom shall I fear? The Lord is the [strength] of my life—of whom shall I be afraid?" Clearly we see that his confidence is in the Lord as his light, salvation, and strength.

In what are you confident? There are many things in life that can erode your confidence. You may not face an entire army like David or be engaged in territorial war like him, but your won issues are not trivial before the Lord. Your confidence should be in God and God alone. David would further declare his confidence in God even in the midst of natural disasters or unimaginable calamities: "God is our refuge and strength, a very present help in trouble. Therefore will not we fear, though the earth be removed, and though the mountains be carried into the midst of the sea; Though the waters thereof roar and be troubled, though the mountains shake with the swelling thereof. Selah" (Ps. 46:1–3, KJV).

No matter what happens, we should not fear and we should be confident. No matter what, we must still trust God. Be confident in him. The writer of the Book of Hebrews says in Hebrews 10:35 (KJV), "Cast not away therefore your confidence, which hath great recompence of reward." There is a great reward for you in your confidence in God. It will be unfortunate to cast away that confidence and jeopardize the sure rewards of God.

God is our refuge and strength. In times of trouble we can call on Him. Things may be shaking all around us. But He is with us and we need not fear. He is our confidence!

PRAYING POINTS

Prayer: *Lord, preserve my life, I pray. Keep me from making mistakes and from falling into the traps and hidden dangers of life. In Jesus's name, amen.*

Prayer: *Lord, You are aware of the circumstances of my life. You know when I sit and when I stand. You know my challenges and my joys. Work things out for me, I pray. In Jesus's name, amen.*

Prayer: *Lord, You are MY faithful God. Thank You for all You have promised to do. I will believe and trust You! In Jesus's name, amen.*

Challenge: *Hold on to God and ask Him to bless you, no matter what you may be facing at the moment.*

Prayer: *Lord, You know what is in my heart and You hear when I call to You. You are my hope and I trust You. In Jesus's name, amen.*

Prayer: *Lord, as I start this new week, I once again affirm my confidence and trust in You, O Lord. I declare that no matter what may come my way, I will hold on to my God. In Jesus's name, amen.*

Prayer: *Lord, I place my life safely into Your hands. I know that You are my refuge and strength, and knowing that You are with me gives me strength. In Jesus's name, amen.*

CONCLUSION

AN YOU CALL on Him whom you do not know? Can you trust Him to attend to you if there is no relationship between you? Though God remains true and faithful to His Word, and will give strength unto those who call on Him, the major problem lies with you.

The story is told of a young man who took an intercontinental flight in an airplane for the first time. He had no idea how things operate in such a flight, and so, when food was brought to him, he refused it because he thought he was going to pay for it from his pocket. He did not know that it was part of the total package for the trip! Was the airline true to its promise? Sure. Whose problem was it, then, that the man did not eat?

In the same manner, the faith of a man brings that man to come near to God and to ask for help. Where that faith is missing, such will not see the need to approach God. Jesus Christ said in John 6:44 that no man can come unto Him except his Father in heaven draws him. There is no other name given under heaven by which man must be saved. If you receive Jesus, you are welcome to the inheritance that He has obtained for you.

Hebrews 4:16 says, "Let us therefore come boldly to the throne of grace, that we may obtain mercy and find grace to help in time of need." Be bold to come before God, for Jesus has made a way for you. Come unto Jesus and then the way shall be made open unto you to receive strength in time of need.

ABOUT THE AUTHOR

A CALL TO THE nations is by the mercy and grace of the Almighty God. This call Samuel Fatoki Sr. yielded his life to pursue, and Everlasting Life Christian Center came to existence in the United States, with churches in Maryland, Virginia, and also in the continent of Africa in Nigeria and Ghana.

Born in Lagos, Nigeria, Apostle Samuel showed exceptional skills in academics and sports and these earned him a scholarship to the United States. He graduated from New Mexico Military Institute in Roswell, New Mexico, with an associate of arts degree in business administration. He later received a bachelor's degree in business management from the University of the District of Columbia and soon furthered his education by securing both master's and doctorate degrees in theology from Canon Bible Institute in Florida.

In 1994, together with his wife, Marcia Fatoki, they started a healthcare company. Pastor Samuel Fatoki was ordained a minister in 1995. He founded the Everlasting Life Christian Center based in Maryland in 2002. Pastor Fatoki is known as an exceptional teacher of God's Word and carries an anointing of miracles with signs following. As a result of this divine gift, he has hosted several successful miracle and healing crusades in Laurel,

Maryland; Brooklyn, New York; and other cities in the United States. These crusades he had taken also to conferences nationally and internationally.

At the Everlasting Life Christian Center, lives are restored, refreshed, revived, and reconnected to God, a place where real miracles occur on a regular basis and deliverance is commonplace for the spiritually oppressed and possessed. There are testimonies of healing of cancer and other major diseases by the power of God. Senior pastor Fatoki says, "My faith in God and the emphasis we place on prayer moves the hand of my Father, He, God, just uses us and we are humbled to be servants of God."

Dr. Samuel Fatoki has been married to co-pastor Marcia Fatoki since 1991 and they have two beautiful children, Samuel Fatoki Jr. and Diamond Fatoki.

CONTACT THE AUTHOR

P.O. Box 1110

Laurel, Maryland 20725

(301) 776-7770

sfatoki@samuelfatokiministries.org